PERSPECTIVE IS
POWER

*Overcoming Adversity and
Embracing a Life Without Limits*

BONUS: 10 EXERCISES INCLUDED TO HELP YOU
LIVE YOUR BEST LIFE.

LIZ BURSTEN

Perspective Is Power © Copyright 2025 Liz Bursten

All rights reserved. No part of this publication may be reproduced, distributed, or transmitted in any form or by any means, including photocopying, recording, or other electronic or mechanical methods, without the prior written permission of the publisher, except in the case of brief quotations embodied in critical reviews and certain other noncommercial uses permitted by copyright law.

The advice and strategies found within may not be suitable for every situation. This work is sold with the understanding that neither the author nor the publisher is held responsible for the results accrued from the advice in this book.

This book is a memoir. It reflects the author's present recollections of experiences over time. Some names and characteristics have been changed, some events have been compressed, and some dialogue has been recreated.

All scripture quotations, unless otherwise indicated, are taken from the Holy Bible, New International Version®, NIV®. Copyright © 1973, 1978, 1984, 2011 by Biblica, Inc™. Used by permission of Zondervan. All rights reserved worldwide. www.zondervan.com The "NIV" and "New International Version" are trademarks registered in the United States Patent and Trademark office by Biblica, Inc™.

ChatGPT (OpenAI) was used by the author for brainstorming purposes only in the reflection sections at the end of each chapter.

ISBN: 979-8-89694-379-2 - Ebook
ISBN: 979-8-89694-380-8 - Paperback
ISBN: 979-8-89694-381-5 - Hardcover

UNLOCK YOUR LIFE WITHOUT LIMITS WITH THIS FREE RESOURCE

Interested in an electronic workbook containing all ten exercises included within this book? Scan the QR Code to download this *free* workbook today!

DEDICATION

To my husband, Spencer. Your presence in my life has been transformative and irreplaceable. I am thankful every day that my journey led me to you and that we get to rock the rest of this beautiful life together.

To our three beautiful sons, Gordon, Teddy, and Jackson. To all three of you, your energy is magic. Your sweet smiles are contagious. You each give life so much more meaning. You are the greatest blessings.

To my parents. You never gave up, and you stood by my side as I navigated through the unthinkable. Your support, patience, and encouragement saw me through the most challenging times. You were the first to teach me that anything is possible.

To my siblings, Joey, Fur, Jay, and Kara. There was a time when the four of you were my sole motivation as I fought for survival. I treasure our memories together and the unique presence we have in each other's lives.

To anyone living with physical or mental challenges, especially those whose conditions were caused by a traumatic incident. You can get through it, with the proper perspective. You already are a beacon of hope to those around you. Keep fighting. Never give up.

To my Lord, Jesus. You have seen me through the darkest times. You have blessed me with more than I could have ever imagined. Thank you.

CONTENTS

Introduction	9
Chapter 1: The Driver's Seat	11
Chapter 2: The Recovery	19
Chapter 3: The Night It Almost Ended	37
Chapter 4: A Second Chance	47
Chapter 5: The One Who Changed Everything	59
Illustrations	69
Chapter 6: A Choice I Never Imagined	91
Chapter 7: When Letting Go Means Living	105
Chapter 8: Hope Against the Odds	115
Chapter 9: Chasing the Challenge	125
Chapter 10: Marathon Mentality	137
Conclusion	151
Appendix A: Liz's Quote Book	153
Appendix B: Resources	157
Acknowledgments	161
About the Author	163

INTRODUCTION

"You want to be in the driver's seat of your own life because if you are not, life will drive you."
—Oprah Winfrey

Life will inevitably throw challenges your way. Everyone will face adversity at some point, but for some of us, the weight of trauma can feel especially overwhelming. If you're reading this, you may have already experienced your own moment of devastation—perhaps a life-altering event that left you questioning everything. Whether you've faced physical, emotional, or spiritual scars, know this: you are not alone in your struggle.

After surviving a catastrophic car accident, I quickly realized the pivotal role perspective plays in overcoming life's most difficult moments. From a near-death experience to the amputation of my leg, life unfolded in ways I never expected. But it was amid this pain that I discovered the power of resilience, hard work, and mindset. With the right perspective and the willingness to persevere, there is nothing you cannot overcome. In this book, I'll show you how your perspective directly influences your journey and how, with the right mindset and determination, you can transform the pain of your past into the strength for a brighter future.

I recently completed my first marathon as a below-knee amputee. For many, this might seem impossible, but through grit and determination, I did it. More than just crossing the finish line, I proved to myself that I can accomplish the unthinkable. I've redefined the limitations others placed on me due to my disability and shattered the world's expectations of what I'm capable of. I turned a life filled with pain and restrictions into one of endless possibilities. And I want you to know—you have that same potential to overcome, grow, and redefine your own limitations.

At the end of each chapter, you'll find an exercise to reflect on. These exercises are designed to help you shift your perspective, build resilience, and take actionable steps toward healing and growth. Invest time and thought into these exercises for a transformative impact on your life. Today is the day you take that first step toward defining your own future. One step at a time, you can rise above your challenges and achieve whatever you set your mind to.

As you read my story, I encourage you to think about your own. Reflect on the ways you've been shaped by your experiences and imagine the life you want to create. As you complete each exercise, dare to dream of a life beyond your current limitations—one that's full of hope, purpose, and endless possibility.

CHAPTER 1

THE DRIVER'S SEAT

"Your hardest times often lead to the greatest moments of your life. Keep going. Tough situations build strong people in the end."
—Roy T. Bennett

Have you ever felt like life just happens to you? Or do you live your life in the driver's seat? Your answers to these questions will determine your future. Think about this for a moment: life doesn't happen *to* you, it happens *because* of you. I have become very familiar with this concept throughout my journey, and I'd love to share that journey with you. All it took was one tiny moment and my life changed forever.

In the very beginning, nothing felt right. I never thought I'd be okay again. But today I am filled and fueled with acceptance and gratitude for everything that happened, exactly how it happened.

The day was Thursday, September 27, 2007, to be exact. I was sixteen years old. I still remember the breeze in the air, the smell of the fall leaves, the warmth of the bright setting sun. After an ordinary day at school followed by tennis practice, I arrived home. I still remember the taste of that orange Gatorade and the guilt I felt for drinking it. I knew it belonged to my little brother, who was saving it for football practice later that week.

I remember the feeling of peace and contentment. There was a calm in my soul that day. I didn't question these feelings at the time, but as I replayed this day in my head over and over for years, I wondered, *Why did those peaceful feelings consume me that day?* It's as if my spirit was preparing my body for what was to come.

This seemingly ordinary day was nearly complete when I realized I had some time to spare before my family got home. My dad was still at work, and my mom was at the store with my siblings gathering some last-minute items to celebrate my heavenly Nana's birthday. Each year on September 27 after my Nana passed, my family would say a cheers on her birthday with root beer floats and send a bouquet of balloons up to heaven.

Knowing I had time before the birthday celebrations began, I hopped in my car and drove two miles down the road to my cousin's house for a quick visit. After I left my cousin's house, my world was never the same again. I can still see my sweet cousin Catherine's face as she waved goodbye when I walked out the front door. Hers was the last face I remembered before waking up in the emergency room.

It was around six p.m., and the sun was perfectly resting on the horizon, symmetrically in the center of the two-lane highway. There was sunshine. There were brake lights. There was a pedal, and the other side of the road felt so close. But it wasn't. That tiny moment I was talking about, when my life changed forever, it happened head-on at fifty miles per hour.

THE DRIVER'S SEAT

The aftermath is just as vivid in my memory today as it was back then. The smell of smoke, rubber, and airbags. The sound of metal crunching, tires squealing, glass shattering, and my own scream. Yes, that's right, my scream. It's like I could hear myself from outside my own body. And then, unexpectedly, the feeling of calm, contentment, and peace.

I recall thinking, *Okay, this just happened, I should call Mom.* As I reached for my cell phone, which was flung to the floor of the passenger seat, my head fell effortlessly and heavily to the steering wheel. I had completely lost feeling and control of my neck. In that moment, my feeling changed. My sense of calm quickly shifted to confusion and worry. I sat with my forehead resting on the steering wheel.

I saw my legs crushed underneath the collapsed dashboard. I noticed bloody layers of skin, burned and peeled away. My eyes filled with tears as my head filled with worry and my heart filled with regret. *What had I just done?*

I vaguely remember the ride in the ambulance. I recall peering out the back window as the road behind us flew by at a blazing speed. I could still smell smoke and rubber as I wondered, *Is everything okay?* I didn't feel pain. I didn't feel scared.

Next thing I knew, I was in the emergency room. This was even more hazy to me. I hardly remember seeing or hearing anything. I do remember some feelings: Chaos. Uncertainty. Confusion. Panic. Calm. It was the strangest combination of feelings. Meanwhile, the lobby was flooding with my family members, friends, tennis teammates, coaches, and even our parish priest.

There is one visual I have from the emergency room. It was my older brother, Joey, standing over my bed. I don't recall what he said or if I said anything, but I just remember looking at him. I remember his eyes. He looked scared. I had never really seen Joey scared, so that was strange. I didn't feel scared at first, but then I started to wonder, *What's really going on? Should I be scared?* I later learned that at this time, our parish priest, Father Paul, performed the Anointing of the Sick, which is often the final sacrament performed just before death.

Suddenly my gurney was rapidly zooming down the hall and into the elevator. Then everything went black. Next thing I knew there was a gust of wind. I felt a slight chill. I was outside. And then it went black again. This was the only memory I have of my transport via Flight for Life. The days and weeks following blurred together, but day by day, I developed more distinct memories.

On the evening of September 27, 2007, Flight for Life had taken me from Kenosha Memorial Hospital to Children's Hospital of Wisconsin and Froedtert & Medical College of Wisconsin, a level one trauma center. Since I was sixteen years old at the time, I was treated for most of my injuries at Children's. The only exception was the treatment of the injury to my right leg, which was handled by the adult physicians at Froedtert. The care I received from both hospitals was exceptional. Since Froedtert is a learning hospital partnered with the Medical College of Wisconsin, there were large teams of doctors working together to treat me. It was incredible.

The morning after the accident, I woke up in my hospital room on the fifth floor in the Medical Surgical Pediatric unit of Children's Hospital. My mom and dad were there. I asked them what happened. They sat down.

"You were in an accident," my mom gently told me as she held my hand. It wasn't until then that I realized my right leg was concealed inside a large white cast. My left leg was covered with bandages. Braces were secured on my neck and back. Tubes were running in and out of my nose, bladder, and both arms.

"What about tennis? I can't miss it this weekend."

The weekend before my accident, I had won the conference championship for girls varsity tennis, No. 1 Singles. The weekend after my accident was the subsectional tournament to qualify for the state championship. I was certain that it was my year to go all the way and win the state championship. Looking back on this moment is funny. I can't believe I thought it would still be possible to play. Clearly, I didn't understand the impact of my injuries. Nor did I recognize the challenging road ahead. Little did I know, the road ahead would be more like a roller coaster.

It wasn't until about sixteen years later, October 8, 2023, to be exact, that I felt like I made it to the "other side" of this thing. This was the day I ran (and finished) the Chicago Marathon as an amputee. After many years of challenges, instability, disappointment, uncertainty, discouragement, pain, limitations, and too many surgeries to count, I made it!

The path to where I am today was not easy. It was filled with countless ups and downs—physically, mentally, and spiritually. However, I can say with resounding certainty today that I would not change a thing. All the pain has given me power to continue onward, always. In more ways than one, I have gone from being unstable to unstoppable—and I am forever grateful for this journey. So please, come along with me as I recollect the journey and all the lessons learned along the way.

My hope in sharing my journey is that you will absorb the same life lessons I've learned, without enduring all the pain. And for the warriors out there who have overcome battles, or perhaps those who are still fighting, my hope is to share common ground with you. The estimated population of the world is over eight billion, and we are all different and unique from each other. How incredible is that? We have so much to share and learn from one another.

After completing my first marathon, I decided right then and there that I was ready to share my story. When I began writing, I asked myself, "What exactly is it that took my experience from an unforeseen trauma to a purposeful life of triumph?" To answer this question, I'd like to highlight one main theme: perspective. Perspective gives you the power to ultimately succeed in whichever challenge or endeavor you are facing. The way in which you look at something is everything.

I'd like to pause for a moment and ask you to reflect on your own journey.

EXERCISE: Current State to Desired State[1]

1. In the Current Problem State box below: Write down three to five challenges you are facing in your life.
2. In the Desired Future State box below: Translate each Current Problem Statement into a Desired Future Statement.
3. In the Barriers box: Write down anything that may come in the way of achieving your Desired Future State.
4. In the Uplifters box: Write down people who may support you in achieving your Desired Future State. Write down experiences that will bring you closer to your Desired Future State.

Current State to Desired State Model	Date:
Current Problem State	**Desired Future State**

---

[1] RyanFriden, "The Desired State," Becoming (blog), ryanfriden.wordpress.com, February 18, 2016, https://ryanfriden.wordpress.com/2016/02/18/the-desired-state.

UPLIFTERS

Write down people and/or experiences that will help you overcome the barriers identified below:

BARRIERS

Write down any barriers that may be in the way of achieving your Future State:

The above exercise is a useful first step in setting personal goals for yourself. You will see the evolution of your thoughts and actions as you continue through further exercises in this book. Each exercise is crafted with the motive to put you in control, no matter what the circumstances. Undoubtedly, life will bring problems, challenges, and adversity. The choice is yours to make. Through all the twists and turns, like it or not, you are in the driver's seat of your own life. Do not be afraid; take the wheel and make it a ride to enjoy!

CHAPTER 2

THE RECOVERY

*"Every day, you reinvent yourself.
You're always in motion. But you decide
every day: forward or backward."*
—James Altucher

Most often recovery comes along with a new reality. A reality in which things change—maybe they slow down, maybe they change direction. I like to look at recovery as a chance to reinvent. There are two milestones in my journey where my recovery led to reinvention: the accident and the amputation. Through recovering from any sort of setback, you are given an opportunity to reinvent yourself, your thoughts, your attitudes, and your personal values.

Before that fateful September day, the day of the accident, my personal values were very different than they are now. Beginning the day after the accident, everything that was important to me began to shift. And this is because, in an instant, my life's purpose shifted. At the age of sixteen, I was filling my days with experiences that fulfilled me.

My focus pre-accident was so simple, yet so full. Completing homework and passing tests. Perfecting my tennis serve. Playing with my siblings. Spending time with my parents. Volunteering as part of my school's Key Club. Enjoying every bit of responsibility as class president. Hanging out with friends. Wondering who would ask me to the Homecoming dance.

And then, the accident happened. None of those things mattered anymore. Instead, my days were filled with troubleshooting problem after problem. I was consumed with fighting to survive. I quickly shifted my focus to what mattered most in life, and everything else faded away. Pre-accident, for example, I was obsessed with perfection. I cared so deeply about what other people thought of me. I wanted to be the best, the brightest, the most accomplished. I sought perfection and acceptance in every aspect of my life. Perfection was a key personal value. Had I continued throughout life this way, my life would look and feel very different today. I was missing something.

Two values that are a large part of who I am today, humility and gratitude, did not play a large role in my life pre-accident.

As the days unfolded post-accident, I was fighting for my life. From stopping the bleeding to repairing the damage to sustaining each treatment, each day had its own set of battles. In the first days, this was a vicious circle going around and around. Did I have time to focus on what anyone else was thinking about me? Did I have time to achieve something great and show off that I was the best? Did I have time to pursue perfection? Absolutely not. Absolutely not. And absolutely not.

As my challenges became greater, my personal values continued to shift in the best possible way. Suddenly the smallest and simplest experiences brought me immense joy.

THE RECOVERY

One of my favorite quotes is by Saint Mother Teresa, "Do small things with great love."[2] At this time in my life, all I could do was small things, but I felt great love and immense gratitude in doing them.

Let me give you a glimpse into this experience and the extent of my injuries. Fractured vertebrae in my neck and lower spine, centimeters away from a vertebrae injury that could have paralyzed me—or worse, it could have killed me in an instant. Shattered right ankle and loss of blood flow to the ankle bone. Burned and gashed knees crushed by the dashboard of my car. Damaged nerves in my right leg, causing any sensation from stone-cold numbness to unbearable burning, tingling, and stabbing pains. Severe liver lacerations, which led to incredible amounts of blood and bile loss. My prognosis was far from great. I was told I would likely never walk again without assistance. Complications from my liver injury nearly took my life.

While in fight-for-life mode, one key value I felt immensely was humility. My life was in the hands of my doctors and nurses, who had the knowledge and resources to help me. My life was in the hands of my parents, who could communicate on my behalf when I was unable to. My life was in the hands of God, who ultimately gave me the chance to *live*! I had one small role to play in all of this: to never give up. And that, I did not.

With humility came an overwhelming sense of empathy and kindness. After relying on others to help me do the simplest things—like eat, bathe, use the bathroom—I never looked at life the same again. I never looked at people the

---

[2] Mother Teresa according to Goodreads Quotes, "Not all of us can do great things. But we can . . .," Goodreads.com, accessed March 19, 2025, https://www.goodreads.com/quotes/6946-not-all-of-us-can-do-great-things-but-we.

same again. I never sought perfection again. And I never felt so free from the feeling of what others were thinking of me. I was alive. But what would this new life become?

I always referred to the date of my accident (September 27) as my Life Day. In fact, my family and I still celebrate it every year. It is something worth celebrating because that is the day that shifted my entire reality and perspective. On that day, I feel as if I were born again. Born into a new life, with newfound values and new potential. Fast-forward nine years to February 25, 2016, when I had my right leg amputated below the knee. I fondly refer to this date as my ampuversary and also my New-Life Day. I will share with you later what ultimately led to this. But for now, I'd like to focus on the aftermath of my amputation as the story has many parallels with my post-accident experience.

Thankfully, I had the luxury of planning for my amputation. I had just married the love of my life, Spencer, the year prior to my amputation. We chose a date to amputate just four months following our wedding. We were certainly living the "in sickness and in health" part of our vows right out of the gate. Of course, going into the amputation was different from the accident, since I knew it was coming. We planned for this over a year in advance. The anticipation and contemplation throughout that time period was far worse than the amputation itself.

Inevitably, the amputation day arrived. We flew down to Oklahoma City to have *the* Dr. William Ertl perform my amputation. A particular method of amputation, called the Ertl Method, is one of Dr. Ertl's specialties as it was invented by his grandfather.

The Ertl Method of amputation creates a bone bridge between the tibia and fibula, which provides a stable foundation to support full weightbearing. This method also uses a technique that promotes the maintenance of tissue with better sensation and blood flow. Ultimately, the Ertl Method results in improved weightbearing, less pain, and more hours of functional prosthetic use. To live the active lifestyle I was dreaming of, I was certain this was the method of amputation that I needed.

On amputation day, we checked into the hospital nice and early. My husband, parents, and one of my brothers were there to cheer me on. As luck would have it, my procedure was delayed several hours due to other emergent cases. The months, weeks, days, and hours of anticipation leading up until that day were so incredibly confusing, conflicting, and emotional. And then the day arrived, and I had to wait. And wait. And wait.

I'm not going to lie, there was a moment in the pre-op triage room where I considered turning my back on this whole thing and going home. But then a feeling of excitement kicked in. Excitement that this could be my last surgery on my right leg. Excitement that, after recovery, I would no longer fall asleep in pain each night and wake up with worse pain the next morning. Excitement that I could finally put the last lingering injury from my accident behind me.

A nurse walked into my room. It was almost show time. After all the waiting and anticipation, it was about to happen. One thing led to the next, and it all moved faster than the speed of light.

As the doctor was inserting my epidural, I squeezed my husband's hands tightly. My heart was pounding in my chest as my eyes flooded with tears. I was scared. The pre-op drugs kicked in, and everything became a bit hazy. Next thing I knew, I was tucked in my bed and wheeling down the hall. We arrived at a large metal door. It opened.

My bed came to an abrupt stop. My blankets were removed from my body. It was cold. The nurse came beside me, guiding my body onto the operating table. Next, the nurse marked an X on my right leg with a marker. I smiled to myself, thinking, *Would they really cut off the wrong leg if they didn't mark it? It's the one with all the scars!* In those few moments lying on the operating table, I remember looking down at my right foot one last time. *Here goes nothing.*

As I examined my right ankle for the last time, I observed how both sides were swollen and covered with scars from every angle. The top was sunken in and deformed. My calf muscle was minuscule, closer to the size of my arm than my other leg.

I thought about the accident. I thought about my wheelchair, casts, crutches, and walking boot. I thought about my shoe inserts, braces, heating pads and ice packs. I thought about all the medication to ease my pain. I thought about the inside of the exam rooms at the Orthopedic Surgery Clinic. I thought about crawling to the shower in the mornings because it hurt too much to walk. I thought about my husband. I thought about our future together. I thought about what my life could become after this. And then everything went dark.

Next thing I knew, I woke up in the recovery room. I had no idea where I was. I looked over and saw my husband and asked, "Is it over yet?"

With a smile on his face, he replied, "It's all done, baby, you did it!" and raised his hand for a high five.

When my hand met his, I felt the most incredible weight lifted off my shoulders. It was a profound sense of happiness and relief—unlike anything I have experienced before. The light at the end of the tunnel was brighter than it had ever been. I thought to myself, *You can only go up from here!*

THE RECOVERY

Yet again, here came another chance to connect with my personal value of humility. This is the beautiful part of adversity hitting repeatedly. If you choose to do so, you will continue to refine and perfect the lessons you've learned. One of my newfound personal values from September 2007, humility, was brought back to center stage as I faced the recovery from my amputation. And this time humility was accompanied by gratitude, empowerment, resilience, and hope.

Immediately following the amputation, my first mission was to make it home to Wisconsin from Oklahoma. Done. My next mission was to rest, recover, repeat. Done. My goal was to be fit for my first prosthetic three months post-amputation. During those three months of acute recovery, I truly sought the opportunity to reinvent myself once again. This time, I wanted to come out on the other side with more strength and capabilities than ever before, mentally and physically.

My recovery post-amputation was very different than any previous recovery I had endured. For one, I knew it was coming. I had the time to mentally prepare. Through research and careful consideration, I was able to anticipate what was to come. But more importantly, I had a different goal in mind. Not only did I want to *get through it*, but I wanted to evolve and rise to the next level in my life. I had already learned the lesson that recovery is a chance to reinvent, and this time I was strategic about it.

After the amputation, while I was physically weak, I was exercising my mental strength daily. I was fortunate to have leave from work for this entire time period while I recovered. At this time, we did not yet have children. I had 100% of my time to focus on myself and my recovery, and it was beautiful. Not only did I want to prepare myself to be strong and active in my prosthetic leg, but I wanted to have the mental strength and capacity of a warrior.

I invested much time and thought into my mindset and attitude. I thought about the connection between my emotions and my reality. Anytime I felt sorry for myself, I would quickly snap myself out of it. I would remind myself of the blessings in my life and the opportunities that lie ahead. Each day I grew closer and closer to that light at the end of the tunnel. I could feel it. I was inspired. I was determined. I was ready.

The accident and the amputation are two happenings in my life that I would call "beautiful disasters." Both jolted my life to a screeching halt. Both caused a shift in my personal values. Both provided me the opportunity to reinvent myself. Looking back on both days, I wouldn't change a thing. As crazy as it sounds, if I had the chance to relive my life, I would make the same choices that led to those two exact things happening to me (the accident and the amputation). Why? Because both of those events in my life played a significant role in shaping the person I have become.

The countless life lessons through each of these events are irreplaceable. You will learn throughout this book that my whole story wasn't always inspiring, exciting, and positive. There were some really (I mean really) tough times. Have you ever heard of rock bottom? Yes, I've been there. In the most challenging of moments with the grimmest circumstances, *that* is where I learned the most.

I bet you're curious about what I learned. I'll tell you . . .

Simply put, the best thing you can do for yourself when trials and tribulations come your way is to take one step at a time. It's that simple. Take one day at a time, one moment at a time. Inevitably, the world will keep moving even if you slow down, and that is great! This used to scare me, that the

THE RECOVERY

world kept moving when my life slowed down. But as soon as I started living in my own bubble and in my own moments, one at a time, that didn't matter to me.

After the accident, it started with the smallest, simplest daily goals. Sitting up in bed for twenty minutes straight, awake. Finishing half of my sandwich at lunchtime and keeping it down. Using my walker instead of my wheelchair to get to the bathroom. Eventually, scooting on my butt to get downstairs to join in family dinner. Showering on my own. Going back to school for half days and then eventually full days. Playing wheelchair tennis. Using crutches full-time. I could go on and on. The reality is, it took a list of probably a million little goals to get me back to normal—well, my new normal.

After my amputation, I had another series of very small daily goals. About two weeks post-amputation, I began with a new morning routine, which included very limited exercise to my arms and core, reading books (self-help) and watching documentaries, showering, and getting ready for my day, even though all I was doing was sitting at home, literally. After a few weeks went by, I discovered this amazing device called an iWalk. It enabled me to bend my knee and strap into the device, weightbearing at the knee, and I could actually walk.

This was a game-changer for my daily routine. I began tracking the minutes and hours I spent walking in it (at Target, the grocery store, outside), just to keep my hips strong. Eventually when I was fitted for my first prosthetic, the prosthetist was amazed at my mobility and hip strength, all thanks to my daily routine in the iWalk! The bottom line is, no matter what you are going through, there are small goals you can set that will take you to the next level. You may not feel the change as you go, but I promise you, one day when you reflect back, you will be amazed!

EXERCISE: Personal Goal Setting[3]

Goal setting is an incredible way to reinvent yourself when facing challenges. Adversity inevitably will change you in one way or another. You might as well take part in the decision-making process: *how* is your adversity going to change you? Think about where you are compared to where you want to be, just for a moment. Then shift your focus only to where you want to be. Think about it. Picture it. Manifest it.

Reference the Desired Future State items listed in your Current to Desired State Model, which you completed in the previous chapter.

1. Copy your Desired Future State items below. Create one goal to achieve each Desired Future State.
2. Copy each goal into its own subsection (e.g., Goal #1 section, Goal #2 section, etc.).
3. For each goal, answer the prompt, "How will I benefit from achieving this goal?" Think about how it will make you feel, why you are motivated to achieve this, and how this will enhance your life.
4. Create subgoals, which are small, attainable steps to achieve this goal. And insert a target date to complete each subgoal.
5. The final step is not included in the template as it will change frequently. Once per week, in a journal or on your phone, wherever you prefer, write or type things you need to do within the current week to work toward each subgoal. You can even break down your to-do list into things you will do today, tomorrow, etc.

---

[3] Jeremy Sutton, scientifically reviewed by Maike Neuhaus, "The Importance, Benefits, and Value of Goal Setting," PositivePsychology.com, December 12, 2024, https://positivepsychology.com/benefits-goal-setting.

THE RECOVERY

| Personal Goal Setting | Date: |

Dessired Future State

Goal
1
2
3
4
5

Goal #1	
My goal:	
How will I benefit from achieving this goal?	
Subgoals (small, attainable steps to achieve this goal):	Target Dates to Complete:
1	
2	
3	
4	
5	
6	
7	
8	
9	
10	

Goal #2

My goal:

How will I benefit from achieving this goal?

Subgoals (small, attainable steps to achieve this goal):	Target Dates to Complete:
1	
2	
3	
4	
5	
6	
7	
8	
9	
10	

Goal #3	
My goal:	
How will I benefit from achieving this goal?	
Subgoals (small, attainable steps to achieve this goal):	Target Dates to Complete:
1	
2	
3	
4	
5	
6	
7	
8	
9	
10	

Goal #4

My goal:

How will I benefit from achieving this goal?

Subgoals (small, attainable steps to achieve this goal):	Target Dates to Complete:
1	
2	
3	
4	
5	
6	
7	
8	
9	
10	

Goal #5	
My goal:	
How will I benefit from achieving this goal?	
Subgoals (small, attainable steps to achieve this goal):	Target Dates to Complete:
1	
2	
3	
4	
5	
6	
7	
8	
9	
10	

Commit to each goal you have written down and you will grow closer and closer to that desired future state. Believe in yourself. As Henry Ford once said, "Whether you think you can, or you think you can't—you're right."[4] You may even surprise yourself and end up in a place greater than what you had imagined.

---

[4] Henry Ford according to Goodreads Quotes, "Whether you think you can, or you think you can't—you're right," Goodreads.com, accessed March 25, 2025, https://www.goodreads.com/quotes/978-whether-you-think-you-can-or-you-think-you-can-t--you-re.

CHAPTER 3

THE NIGHT IT ALMOST ENDED

"If you lose faith, you lose all."
—Eleanor Roosevelt

One of my favorite principles in life is the 90/10 rule. The 90/10 rule is a concept that states 10 percent of life is made up of what happens to you, and 90 percent is determined by how you react to those events. What happened to me in October of 2007 is an example of the 90/10 rule in action. I don't remember exactly what the date was, but I have some very specific memories from this day that are crystal clear. This is my story of the night it almost ended.

Some days had passed since the accident. At this point, I had several surgeries and procedures to stabilize my condition, but I wasn't getting better. I remember waking up in the middle of the day. The sun was shining brightly through my hospital room window. My mom was there, she always was. In fact, Mom rarely ever left my side. And when she did, my dad was there in her place. Looking back on this particular day, I am certain I would not have survived if I didn't have my parents by my side to fight for my life when I needed it most.

At one point that day, the sun just perfectly hit my eyes in a way that brought back very real memories and feelings of the crash. It was like a nightmare, but I was completely awake. I was still very weak, so I didn't talk much. Then a nurse walked into my room and placed her hands on my bed railing. She began speaking to me about my medicines, my catheter, and something about drain output. All of this talk caused me to feel very overwhelmed.

As the nurse spoke, she moved her hands up and down, touching the bed rail every other word. That hurt my body immensely. Just the tiniest movement of her hand touching my bed sent waves of throbbing pain from my head to my toes.

Excruciating pain coursed through my lower back and my entire abdomen. After giving birth many years later, I can compare the pain I felt that day to active labor contractions. It was the worst pain I had ever felt.

As the day went on, those pains would come and go. All the while, my stomach was expanding more and more by the hour. I looked like I was about to give birth! I realized the nurses and doctors were stopping by more frequently. I noticed quiet conversations going on among the medical team near my doorway. The pain continued to get worse, and my stomach continued to expand. After an x-ray and CT scan, the medical team was certain that my abdomen was filling with blood. I was bleeding internally, or so they thought. Eventually, I drifted off to sleep again and slept the rest of the day away.

Suddenly I woke up and yanked the NG tube out of my nose and throat. I ripped off my hospital gown and pulled out my pic line just as quickly. I don't remember all of this, but later I learned that I was beginning to bleed from every cavity in my body. My ears and nose were dripping with blood. The containers collecting the output from my NG tube and catheter turned red. My stark white sheets were now soaking and red.

THE NIGHT IT ALMOST ENDED

I remember part of this experience as if I were outside of my own body, looking down at myself. My body was thrashing and thrusting around as the nurses ran in and tried to keep me from ripping every other tube out of my body. I felt sorrow and pity for myself. I felt ashamed and dark. I wanted to curl up in a ball and give up. I wanted nothing more than for this pain to stop. So I closed my eyes.

I vividly remember that split second when I shut my eyes. My heavy eyelids slowly closed. The pain subsided. I felt scared for just a moment. Then I remember peace. Silence. Relief.

I felt warm and comfortable. I was content and happy. I actually remember feeling a sensation of the warm, bright sun shining on my face; but it was nighttime, and the sun was nowhere to be found.

I don't remember seeing or hearing anything; it was just a feeling. This feeling was something special, something unique. I liked it. Slowly the feeling of peace started to slip away. I remember a moment when my curiosity burst in. *What is this peace I am feeling? Why do I suddenly feel comfortable? Where did my pain go? What is happening to me?*

And then, BOOM! I was back in the pain, misery, and chaos. I felt every bit of pain. I saw the worried eyes of my dad as my medical team hustled around the room. *Am I dying?*

As I felt my life slipping away from me, all four of my siblings' faces popped into my mind. My older brother, Joey, the only person I remember seeing immediately following my accident. He told me I would be okay. Joey and I are nineteen months apart; we spent our whole childhood together. I thought about how incomplete life would feel if Joey were to disappear. I couldn't do that to him. *C'mon Liz, you can't leave Joey behind!*

I thought of my little brother, Fur, who looked at me like I was the greatest superhero at his last football game, when I arrived just in time with the after-game snacks for his team. I loved cheering for my siblings at their games; it was one of my favorite parts of being a sister. *C'mon, Liz, you can't miss the kids' games!*

I thought of my little brother, Jay, who made the coolest sound effects when playing with his action figures. Jay always had the most unique collections of toys, and I loved playing with him. He and Fur gave me an excuse to act like a kid a little bit longer. *C'mon, Liz, you have to stick around to play with the boys!*

I thought of my little sister, Kara, who loved anything girly. Kara was in kindergarten at this time, and my last memory with Kara before the accident was an after-school tea party, with Kara's fluffy teapot, plush muffins, and squishy teacups. *C'mon, Liz, you have to be there for Kara. She can't grow up without a sister!* These thoughts preoccupied my mind from the pain for a while.

As these thoughts consumed me, I felt a fire inside. Nothing was going to put that fire out. This is when I shifted my thoughts to prayers. I was begging the Lord to let me live. I would not give up. I would not give up. I would not give up. After all, life is only 10 percent what happens and 90 percent how you react. I chose to react with faith, belief, hope, and a fight. I had such a strong belief in my ability to get through this. I had faith that God had greater plans for me and would let me live. All I could do was continue to believe and continue to fight.

What happened next was divine intervention at its finest. My vitals were unstable and rapidly declining. My doctors were certain the fluid they saw in my scans was blood and weren't quick to operate as the source of the bleed wasn't obvious. The medical team took time in deliberating what the next steps would be.

THE NIGHT IT ALMOST ENDED

I don't remember this part, but my Papa called my mom urging her to tell the doctors that all I needed was a stent placed in my liver to drain the bile. My Papa was so certain my abdomen was filling with bile due to my liver injury, not blood. I should note, my Papa was not a medical professional. His expertise came from the fact that this is exactly what happened to his wife, my Nana, just before she died. My liver prognosis was identical to my Nana's, and he knew exactly what needed to be done.

One thing led to the next, and my mom convinced the lead surgeon on my case to operate and insert stents. I have very limited memory leading up to this surgery, but I later learned the procedure was life-threating and extremely delicate due to my neck injury. This is why the doctors were hesitant to operate when they initially thought I was bleeding out. Intubating me and moving my C-spine a minuscule amount could have paralyzed or killed me.

Interestingly enough, one of my mom's cousins was also a surgeon at Froedtert and could oversee the entire procedure and keep my parents informed. My parents, siblings, friends, and extended family relentlessly prayed for me as I underwent this surgery. Thankfully, I pulled through, and the surgery was a remarkable success. It turned out my Papa's advice was right. From that point on, I turned the corner. Things were looking up.

The power of prayer plays a significant role in my success through adversity. From the very first moment of my accident, the ripple effect of prayer began. It began with phone calls and messages cascading throughout my network of family and friends to pray that God spare my life. It expanded to my church and school communities. The day after my accident, nearly my entire high school, students and faculty, gathered at the school chapel. I was told the chapel was filled with standing room only as everyone joined together in prayer. My parents received countless cards and messages that prayer chains all across the country were ongoing in my name.

The outpouring of prayer was incredible. The power of the human spirit is also incredible. My strong belief and desire to live gave me the extra strength I needed to get through those moments.

I am fueled by my belief that perspective is power. But perspective paired with *prayer* is a superpower. When reflecting on the night it almost ended, I realize that peace I felt in the midst of the pain and agony was someone from above—God, an angel, maybe even my Nana. It was a presence. On that night I felt like I was not alone. Someone was up there fighting with me, fighting *for* me.

Every single day after that night, I spent hours of my days in prayer. Sometimes I'd say formal prayers, like the rosary or chaplet, but often I would just talk to God. Naturally, I was asking for a lot from God: to help me get through this, to help me be strong again, to take the worries about me away from my family and let them feel happy, and so on and so forth.

Of the many asks I had for God, my favorite was this: to help me find a purpose in all of this, to make my suffering meaningful. As soon as I started asking those questions, my mentality shifted. For example, now when I'd go into a painful procedure, instead of praying to God, "I need this, help me with that, me, me, me," I was then reflecting on who in my life, or who in the world, I could pray for. And then I prayed for them. My suffering became meaningful.

On the night it almost ended, it became evidently clear to me that this life was bigger than anything in my own control. I am certain I would not be alive today if I didn't choose faith. So yes, we must believe in ourselves. But we also must believe in something greater. Have faith.

EXERCISE: Faith Reflection

This next exercise is a prompt for journaling. Depending on your faith and beliefs, you may alter the questions as desired. The intention of this exercise is to recognize that there is a greater purpose for the direction of our lives. I believe God is in charge. Do you believe in a higher power? Have you felt the strength of this power at any point in your life? Personally, I have found that when I combine my faith and belief in God with the mental strength discussed in this book, anything is possible and the best version of myself can shine through.

Determine a frequency that works for you: daily, every other day, weekly, etc. Per your determined frequency, write down your response to the following questions.

FAITH-FOCUSED SELF-REFLECTION
1. What happened today?
2. Where did you see a higher power at work in others or in you?
3. What did you learn today?
4. What are you thankful for?
5. How are you feeling emotionally?
6. How did you fall short of loving others or yourself?
7. What are you asking of a higher power to do in you and through you?
8. What can you do more in return?
9. What will you do tomorrow to move forward in alignment with your religious beliefs?
10. Who in your life could use prayers right now? And how will you pray for them?

THE NIGHT IT ALMOST ENDED

On the night it almost ended, God brought me peace in the moments I could not control. I believe God created me with a very particular amount of strength and optimism to get through everything life has thrown my way. I also believe God has given me free will to make choices. So now the ball is back in my court. I must choose to believe in myself. And I must choose to exercise optimism.

It's my choice to strengthen my mind, body, and spirit to make the most of my life. I survived the night it almost ended. I woke up in the morning feeling like I'd dodged a bullet. Enough was enough. I was all in and ready to fight for my life. And I didn't just want to merely be alive, I wanted to live my best life and give all the glory to God when I succeeded. I believed in myself and had faith in the Lord. From that moment on, each day felt like a gift. This experience truly put things into perspective.

C'mon, Liz, I thought to myself, *let's make the most of this life.*

CHAPTER 4

A SECOND CHANCE

"Life doesn't get easier or more forgiving, we get stronger and more resilient."
—Steve Maraboli

The year was 2011, and summer was soon approaching. I had completed almost four semesters at my dream school, Saint Mary's College of Notre Dame in South Bend, Indiana. I completed "almost" four semesters as I actually headed home early and did not complete the final exams for my sophomore year spring semester. I was so close to the finish line for that year, but I simply couldn't go on any longer.

From the accident until this point, there was much hope and momentum, but during my sophomore year, everything changed. I was still living in chronic pain, continuing to battle illness and injury while trying to be "normal" like everyone else. Behind the scenes of my physical battle, I was fighting an emotional and psychological battle in silence. I was ashamed to let anyone know how I truly felt. No one would understand what I was really thinking and feeling, at least that's what

I told myself. In April 2011, I experienced a psychological breakdown. Everything felt too heavy. Nothing made sense. I began to unravel. I was falling apart.

As this unraveling began, I recalled my doctors' advice while I was inpatient post-accident. They recommended I seek treatment for Post-Traumatic Stress Disorder (PTSD). I never did, nor did I have time or energy to at that time. Fast-forward to June 2011. Summertime was usually welcomed with excitement and fun plans, but this one felt different for many reasons. After my unfinished semester, I was preparing to go in for yet another ankle surgery. My previous ankle surgery earlier that year took a piece of my tibia and implanted it within my talus (ankle bone).

The goal was for the live bone to revascularize my dead talus bone. But just like many other treatments to my ankle, it was unsuccessful. Instead of helping me, the surgery left me at a deficit, with a mass in the center of my talus. The bone graft from my own body did not take. And this is what led to my surgery in June 2011, a simple repair with more screws and more hardware. Easy. This was my seventh ankle surgery in four years. It felt routine at this point. But there was nothing routine about what I had planned.

The night before and morning of my surgery, I took what I thought was just the right amount and the right combination of pills to cause an overdose when combined with the anesthesia. I made it to the hospital, bright and early, on surgery day. I was ready for my life to end. To be honest, I don't really remember much of that morning. But I do remember waking up after surgery, realizing my plan had failed.

I won't get into the details, but let's just say I was extremely sick. I couldn't control my body. I was sweating and then shivering and then sweating again. I was anxious beyond belief. I wanted to crawl out of my skin. I felt so low, so miserable, so defeated, so confused. My head was pounding, and the room was spinning.

I remember my surgeon's usual visit post-op never happened. As a frequent flyer in the orthopedic surgery unit, I knew that was unusual. I remember feeling ashamed, wondering if everyone in the OR knew what I was trying to pull. I remember hating myself for wanting to die. I remember feeling thankful that it didn't work. I remember realizing that I had a problem, and it was seriously time to tell someone about it. It was time for help.

When I arrived home from the hospital later that day, I decided to pull out my journal and read some of my past entries. I wanted to remind myself of all that I have gone through. I wanted to remember how extraordinary I used to feel about being alive, and how thankful I was for my life. *How did it come to this?*

As I read, I realized the back-and-forth conflict I had had with myself. It's interesting, going through my journey day by day. So much was happening. Focusing on the positive kept me strong. But at the same time, I wasn't giving enough time or credit to the challenges. I didn't allow myself to properly process the negative feelings, which ultimately wasn't healthy.

When I came across a poem I wrote, I noticed how it perfectly depicted this conflicting balance between the positive and negative. Then halfway through the poem, there was a shift. As I read the second half of the poem, a chill ran down my spine. I could feel the strong sense of self-belief I had back then. And I could feel that self-belief deep within as I sat there in bed. I was confident that I had it within myself to overcome every single piece of adversity this accident has caused me—even the psychological part.

10/23/2008

Colors fade, seasons change
People come and go.
What if I could stop the world?
Then maybe I would know.

I'd know how to live my life,
I'd be strong, healthy, and free.
Suddenly I'm feeling trapped,
But that's my life, that's me.

I live my life, a constant struggle,
Why am I still here?
If God did love me, He'd come and take me,
He'd rid me of my fear.

My fear to go, my fear to stay,
My fear to love, my fear to hate.
I'm stuck, I'm trapped inside this bubble,
Why live life with so much trouble?

Stop. Listen.

Suddenly the winds have changed.
Can my life be rearranged?
"You must try,"
I hear the voice inside me cry.

A SECOND CHANCE

It's okay if I stumble,

That will merely keep me humble.

And it's okay if I fall,

Because I will never lose it all.

Now I see the budding on the trees,

And I feel the calm within the seas.

I realize—that's still me, deep within.

And that "me"—she's tough, she always wins.

She climbs and rises to the top.

She lives life to the fullest, and she won't stop!

Believe! Believe! Believe in YOU!

Faith and hope will see you through.

If she can do it, you can too.

    I read that last stanza of the poem over and over and over again. I thought to myself, *Believe in yourself, Liz!* Reading this poem reignited the steadfast belief in myself I'd always had. In that moment, lying in my bed, I made a commitment to myself. From that moment on, I would cheer myself on. No more feeling sorry for myself. No more negative self-talk. No more losing belief. In the months leading up to my suicide attempt, I had lost my way. The biggest piece I had lost was the belief in myself. This poem highlighted the shift in perspective I needed.

    To follow through with this commitment to myself, beginning the very next day, I started each morning with positive affirmations. The positive affirmations served as reminders to keep believing in myself. I would write these affirmations with a dry-erase marker on my mirror. It would be the first thing I would read at the beginning of my day and the last thing I'd read at the end of my night. But that wasn't enough. In between those beginning and ending moments of each day, I made a conscious effort to think positively about myself and my journey.

The easiest way to keep my perspective heading in the right direction was to foster an attitude of gratitude. At any moment when negative thoughts or feelings crept into my mind, I would acknowledge them, take a breath, and immediately think about one thing I was grateful for. And day by day, I transformed myself. Fewer of those negative thoughts would enter my mind.

Eventually, I didn't have to try very hard to think positively. It became part of me. My new default feelings were strong, optimistic, and full of hope. Yes, me, the same person who tried to take her own life—in a short amount of time, I turned around and became someone who loved her life and loved herself. Perspective gave me power!

I'd like to share with you one of my favorite stories about perspective:[5]

> One day an old Cherokee man sits down with his grandson to teach him about life.
> "A fight is going on inside of me," he says to the boy. "It's a terrible fight between two wolves. One is evil—he is full of rage, jealousy, arrogance, greed, sorrow, regret, lies, laziness, and self-pity."

---

[5] Mateo Soul, "The Two Wolves Story (What It Really Means)," The Art of Healing, theartofhealing.com.au, August 25, 2020, https://theartofhealing.com.au/2020/08/the-two-wolves-story-what-it-really-means/.

> He continues, "The other is good—he is filled with love, joy, peace, generosity, truth, empathy, courage, humility, and faith. This same fight is going on inside the hearts of everyone, including you."
>
> The grandson thinks about this for a few minutes, and then asks his grandfather, "Which wolf wins?"
>
> The old Cherokee simply replies, "The one you feed."

I have never found a story that has resonated with me as much as this one. Whichever wolf you feed will win! During that dark time of my life in 2011, I was most definitely feeding the evil wolf. My negative thoughts turned into negative actions and were creating a sad life. But right when I shifted my mindset, right when I began feeding the good wolf, the most incredible things began happening in my life. Whatever you tell yourself, you're right! So why not feed your mind with all things good and positive? Feed the good wolf. Let perspective be your power.

EXERCISE: Dear Future Self

Follow the steps below to write a letter to your future self.[6] This exercise is incredibly powerful in acknowledging exactly where you are today while envisioning where you want to go. Repeating this exercise annually, or at whichever frequency you decide, will serve as an accountability tool. You will be amazed at the changes and progress between each letter. I hope you find the same value in this exercise as I have!

| Dear Future Self | Date: |

Step 1

Start by deciding when you want your future self to read the letter.

My recommendation is to write a letter to your future self once per year. However, perhaps you are working really hard on achieving significant changes in a shorter timeframe. Then you may want to consider writing to yourself more frequently. At whichever frequency you determine to write to yourself, open and read your letter from the previous time period before beginning to write your new letter.

---

[6] Celena Hathaway and Luke Smith, "How to Start a Letter to Your Future Self: What to Say & Include," wikiHow.com, updated September 12, 2024, https://www.wikihow.com/Write-a-Letter-to-Your-Future-Self#:~:text=Summarize%20yourself%20in%20the%20present.%20Who%20are%20you%3F,wanted%20to%20do%3F%20Ask%20your%20future%20self%20questions.

Step 2

Keep your letter casual. **Write to yourself as if you are writing to a friend.**

Option 1: When talking about your current self, write in first person ("I" language). When talking about your future self, write in second person ("you" language).

Option 2: Or refer to yourself in third person ("he/she/they"). This will read more like a self-reflection but may help you talk about yourself more objectively.

Step 3

Now the writing begins! Tell your future self about your current situation. **Remind yourself who you currently are and exactly what your situation is.** How do you spend your time each day? What do you enjoy (e.g., particular movies, books, hobbies)? Who are your closest friends? What challenges are you facing? **Reference important life events.** Did you recently move, or are you planning to? Are you graduating or starting a new job? Are you in a relationship? Has something in your health changed?

Step 4

Describe your worries and fears. **Write about fears or shortcomings you may have,** such as speaking in front of a group, starting a new job, or moving to a new town. This will make it easy to identify in the future if you've overcome these fears. This may also prompt you to strategize and problem-solve to begin overcoming those fears or shortcomings. **Write about mistakes you've made or things you may be ashamed of but can't tell anyone else about.** Do you struggle with vices or bad habits? Did you handle a situation poorly and you know you could have done better? Remember, your future self is your friend and your role model. They're a smarter, more experienced version of you.

Step 5

Identify your key values and beliefs. Write about your own experiences and what guides the current you. Your beliefs play a large role in your actions. Writing down your current beliefs and values can help shape your ideas of who you want to become. Do you have religious beliefs? What values or morals guide you (e.g., helping others in need, always being kind)?

Step 6

Describe your skills and abilities. **Write about your skills and strengths in your current life.** The more skills and abilities, the better. Writing down these positive pieces of yourself will help propel you forward as you strive to achieve your goals.

Step 7

Define your goals and dreams. Write about the goals you'd like to accomplish between now and the time you plan to read the letter. Do you want to start a family? Do you want a change in career? Are there new skills or abilities you want to acquire? Are there changes to yourself, family, society, or environment you want to see?

QUICK TIP: Write to yourself things you want to stop, start, and continue.

Step 8

Ask your future self questions. Do you like your job? Are you in love? Have you realized your dreams? Are you happy? NOTE: These should be open-ended questions left for your future self to answer. If this isn't your first letter to your future self, answer the questions you asked yourself in your previous letter here too!

Step 9

Set a calendar reminder to open the letter in one year (or in whichever frequency you determined in step one). Write to yourself each year. This is a great tool to reflect on progress and identify where to continue work and where to focus next.

Writing a letter to your future self is a great way to use perspective to your advantage. When you take an active approach to positively influence your outcome, positivity will inevitably follow. If perspective is power, imagine how powerful a positive perspective can be.

CHAPTER 5

THE ONE WHO CHANGED EVERYTHING

"Sometimes the bad things that happen in our lives put us directly on the path to the best things that will ever happen to us."
—Nicole Reed

I've been all over the spectrum of optimism versus pessimism. I've had a history of "aha" moments where I'd rediscover and reinvent my belief in self, but it wasn't until a certain person came into my life that this became a fiber within my being. As you learned in the previous chapter, the summer of 2011 was a huge turning point where I focused on mastering my own mind.

This was previously an area of untapped potential. After years of reacting to everything happening to me, I lost sight of the fact that I could control my outcome. All I had to do was purposely, consistently, and actively choose to embrace a positive attitude.

It was a beautiful summer day, July 9, 2011, to be exact. This was just three short weeks after the surgery where I tried to end it all, which I now refer to as "the incident." While I cherished my life after surviving that experience, I was still stuck in a blurred, confused state. The positive changes I was striving for didn't just happen overnight. I had a long road ahead of me to "make my comeback." Naturally, the long road came with a fair share of ups and downs. It is quite remarkable that I found the motivation to leave my home on that fateful day in July, so soon after the incident.

My cousin Jacklynne was having a birthday party at her parents' house that evening. My best friend and cousin, Cynthia, convinced me to go with her. I hobbled out of bed and got myself ready to go. This was the first social gathering I was attending since the incident. It felt good to get dressed nice, fix my hair, and do my makeup. I still couldn't walk, but I felt comfortable enough getting around on my crutches. And my crutches were ready to party too—I had decorated them years before with hot pink and leopard-print duct tape. I didn't quite feel like myself, but I sure did start to feel like me again on this night. I was excited about something for the first time in a while.

Something I've failed to mention so far is that I come from a uniquely large family. I am one of sixty-seven first cousins, just on my mom's side. Thirty-five of us cousins lived in the same hometown and grew up right alongside each other. We went to the same schools, celebrated birthdays and holidays together, and some of us were inseparable, seeing each other on an almost-daily basis. So naturally, most guests at my cousin Jacklynne's birthday party were our relatives.

When I arrived at the party, I quickly joined the circle around the bonfire. I figured I'd find somewhere to sit and put my leg up. Next thing I knew, there were some non-relatives joining the party. This was unexpected. As I mentioned, it

THE ONE WHO CHANGED EVERYTHING

was common for our gatherings to consist of family members with just a few familiar friends sprinkled into the mix.

Several of my cousins attended the University of Wisconsin-Parkside (UWP), located in Kenosha, and they invited some of their friends from the UWP soccer team—the soccer guys. When the soccer guys joined us, a group of us greeted them, and we all began playing flippy cup together. I managed to play, balanced on one leg with my crutches propped against the tree beside me. I felt silly hobbling around on my crutches, but boy am I happy that I chose to do so.

Shortly after we started playing the game, one of the soccer guys walked over and stood right beside me as he asked to join my team. He introduced himself to me as Spencer B. Immediately I was drawn to this guy. And it wasn't just his cute smile or the way he wore his white hat backwards. It was his energy, his spirit, his personality. Something inside me felt a pull to him.

When he asked to join my team, inside I was screaming yes! But I awkwardly replied, "I'm not sure, we're on a roll and have won three straight games. Are you any good?"

"All I do is win!" he said and stepped right up to the table.

After the first round of flippy cup with Spencer on my team, he noticed my crutches. Naturally this led to the "what happened" conversation. I shared with Spencer a few details about my accident but purposely didn't elaborate too much. We continued to chat about our families, school, and random things. The best part about this conversation was that Spencer saw me. He didn't focus on the fact that I was injured or recovering. At this point in time, I was feeling so consumed by my physical and psychological challenges. But when I was with Spencer, none of that mattered. I got to be Liz again!

As the night went on, we were all having a blast playing games and chatting around the bonfire. I went inside to use the restroom and ended up visiting with my Papa for quite some time. When I returned outside, Spencer B and the soccer guys were gone. Luckily, Spencer and I had already exchanged phone numbers. Little did I know at the time, but meeting Spencer would change my life forever in the best way possible.

After having a few too many drinks throughout the night, I felt courageous enough to text Spencer. I said, "Spencer B, come back!" But I didn't hear anything until the next morning when he responded, "Who's this?" I felt so embarrassed that I had texted him.

We laughed it off, and today he admits that he knew exactly who I was and was playing "hard to get." The day after that text exchange, I was admitted into the hospital for extensive inpatient treatments, lasting just under three weeks. I didn't hear from Spencer during that time, nor did I have a reason to reach out to him.

My inpatient treatments were complete, and I was finally able to go home. On the day I went home, I invited two cousins and two friends over for a bonfire. As we were sitting around the fire at my parents' house, my phone buzzed. It was a text message. I opened my phone and read from Spencer B, "Hey! What are you up to tonight?" I was so excited to hear from him but a little nervous about what to say or do next.

I went with my gut feeling and invited him to join us. And he did! Spencer and one of his friends joined us; naturally it was one of the soccer guys from the night we met. That night after Spencer left, he was the one to text me. I guess he wasn't playing hard to get after all! The very next day, we went on our first date, and the rest is history.

THE ONE WHO CHANGED EVERYTHING

After that first date, we hardly went for more than a day without seeing each other. We fell in love and were instantly buddies. As I am writing today, it has been thirteen years and nine months since that fateful night we met. We have been married for nine years and counting! Even though I still feel like our story is just beginning, we have already realized some of our greatest dreams together.

More importantly, we have already navigated through considerable challenges together as well. When I reflect on our story, from the moment we met until now, I truly believe we are soulmates. We were made for each other. We complete each other. And without him, my life would not be the beautiful masterpiece it is today.

This may sound like such an ordinary love story, and in a way, it is. During our college years, Spencer once said to me, "There's no such thing as an ordinary moment; every moment is extraordinary." And that's true. Therefore, our love story is extraordinary. Our life is extraordinary. From the big moments to the small moments and everything in between. Extraordinary.

I truly believe this today, but the interesting thing is, I didn't fully buy in to this concept when I first heard it from Spencer. But he believed it, he acted like it, he lived it! From the very first day we met, I was constantly amazed by his personality: always cheerful and upbeat. And I'm serious. Always. I remember thinking to myself, *How can someone be this happy, all the time?* The most ordinary occurrences with Spencer always felt fun and exciting. Whether we were running errands, doing homework, making dinner, cleaning the dishes, or driving to school, we were always having a blast!

As I was facing many personal challenges when Spencer and I first met, he treated me with compassion and kindness. But at the same time, he never felt sorry for me. Spencer believed in me and empowered me to be the best version of myself, no matter what. This is where my love for the special "Spencer energy" comes from. In Spencer's eyes, every single moment is extraordinary. And let me tell you, when I'm with Spencer, he makes me realize that too.

Very early on in our relationship, he introduced me to one of his favorite books, *You Are What You Think* by David Stoop, PhD. This book focused on one key principle: Attitude is everything. The book specifically teaches you how to use positive self-talk to make positive changes in your attitudes and beliefs, and thus your life. Spencer always says, "If you think you can, you're right. If you think you can't, you're right." The more I got to know Spencer, the more I realized how much he embodied every teaching in that book.

Aside from my own relationship with Spencer, the presence he has in others' lives is what astounded me at first. The number of friends and loved ones in his life is truly amazing. To this day, I am in awe of the impact he has on the world. To have an abundance of people who care for you and for you to care for is something special. Spencer will make friends with the guy in line at the gas station or the waiter at the restaurant. His positive outlook yields such an incredibly positive life, and you can feel it just by being around him. I am incredibly blessed to spend this life with him. But perhaps the greatest blessing is that God placed us together exactly when He did.

Of course, when Spencer first popped into my life, I was in the process of what I affectionately refer to as "mounting my comeback." In the months before meeting him, I was at an all-time low mentally. But in the weeks before meeting Spencer, I was determined to reinvent myself, stronger and better than ever before. I was determined to overcome. I was determined to mount a comeback. And suddenly Spencer appeared and taught me some of the most valuable lessons I've learned!

Although I wanted to, I didn't truly and fully absorb his unwavering optimistic mindset right away. This is something that didn't come easy to me right away. I learned so much from Spence during our first year together. I realized a piece of myself that was missing. My outlook was poor and my mindset was weak, and I needed to strengthen both of those pieces if I were to truly move forward in my life.

During those critical days and weeks when I was mounting my comeback, Spencer's outlook changed mine in the best possible way. It's as if his outlook is contagious. Today, like Spencer, I too believe that anything is possible. I too believe that there is no such thing as an ordinary moment and that every moment is extraordinary.

After falling to an all-time low point in my journey post-accident, I was led directly into the path of my soulmate. Every wrong turn I took earlier that year led me exactly to where I was meant to be. Had I not met Spencer when I did, I wouldn't be who I am today. I would still be missing that unwavering belief that I can control my outcome by maintaining a positive attitude, always.

The year 2011 started in a very dark place, but by the time the year ended, my outlook was bolder and brighter than ever. When you feel you are in the darkest moments of your battle, don't give up! Keep going and find the light. It's out there! Put yourself out there. And your light may shine through at the most unexpected time.

EXERCISE: Positive Affirmations[7]

Complete the following phrases with positive affirmations for yourself. **QUICK TIP:** Write the prompts (i.e., "I AM . . .", "I CAN . . .") on your bathroom mirror, or on a Post-it. Fill in the blank with a new response each day. During the ups and downs of your day, recite that affirmation to yourself!

Positive Affirmation	Date:

DAILY REMINDER

I AM . . .

I CAN . . .

I WILL . . .

I AM PROUD OF . . .

IT'S OKAY TO . . .

---

[7] The Essential Boomer, "Positive Affirmation Worksheet" (PDF), hmi.org, 2015, https://hmi.org/wp-content/uploads/2020/12/Positive-Affirmation-Worksheet.pdf.

THE ONE WHO CHANGED EVERYTHING

Now you are called to engrain each of those positive affirmations into your mind. Think about them daily. Be a living example of these affirmations. Remember, a positive attitude can change everything.

ILLUSTRATIONS

Local

Two hurt in head-on accident

A Pleasant Prairie firefighter pours absorbent material to soak up automobile fluids at the scene of a head-on accident on the 5600 block of 104th Street on Thursday evening. Elizabeth Clark, 18, the driver of a 1999 Buick Century, was taken to Kenosha Medical Center. Guy Griffin, 42, the driver of an Audi TT, was taken to St. Catherine's Medical Center. Both drivers were severely injured in the crash, said officials with the Pleasant Prairie Police Department. According to authorities, the Buick Century crossed the center line into oncoming traffic, striking the Audi head-on. The driver of a Dodge Caravan, who had attempted to avoid the accident, was not hurt. Clark was cited for inattentive driving. The setting sun may have been a factor in the accident, authorities said.

September 28, 2007 — A clipping from the Kenosha newspaper published the day after the accident, capturing the early details surrounding the incident.

LIZ BURSTEN

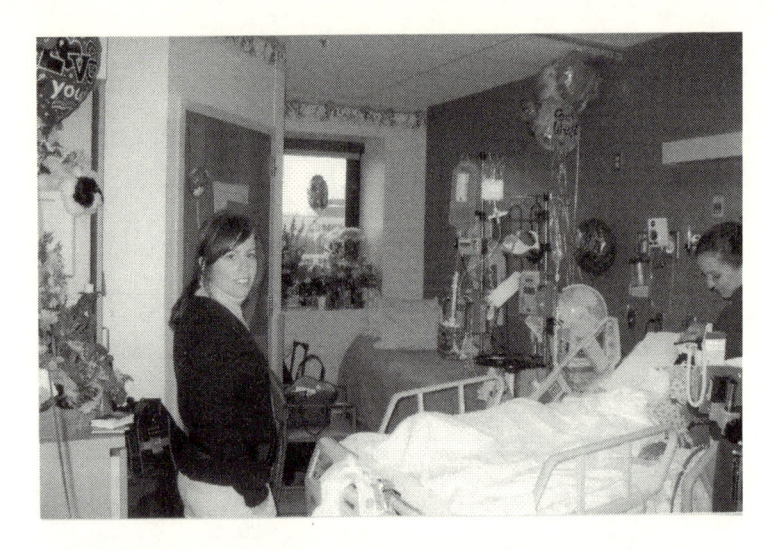

September 29, 2007 — In the days following the accident, I was in critical condition. Flight for Life transported me from Kenosha Medical Center to Children's Hospital of Wisconsin immediately following the accident. My mom never left my side.

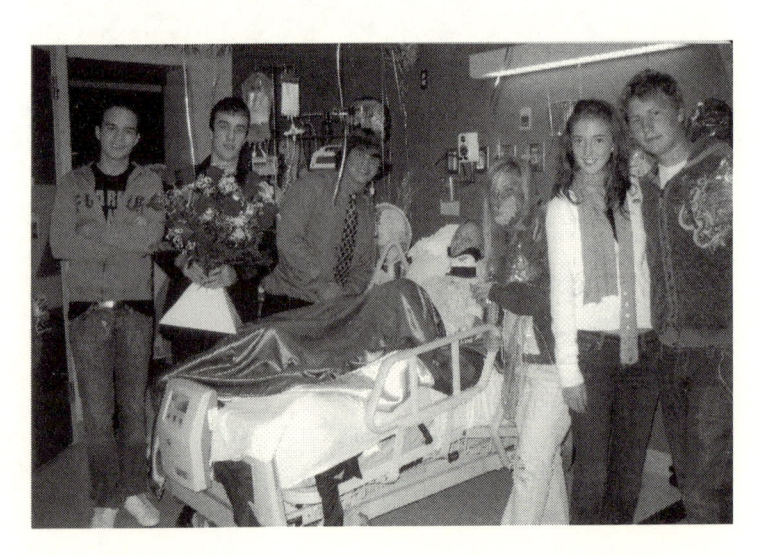

October 13, 2007 — Still recovering and unable to attend the Homecoming dance, I was surprised with a celebration at the hospital. Pictured here are Billy (friend), Joey Clark (brother), Justin (cousin), Sarah (cousin), Bailey (friend), and Nick (cousin).

ILLUSTRATIONS

October 13, 2007 – Surrounded by friends and family in the hospital, I celebrated Homecoming in my own way. Since I couldn't wear my dress, my mom brought a special, shiny purple blanket to mark the occasion.

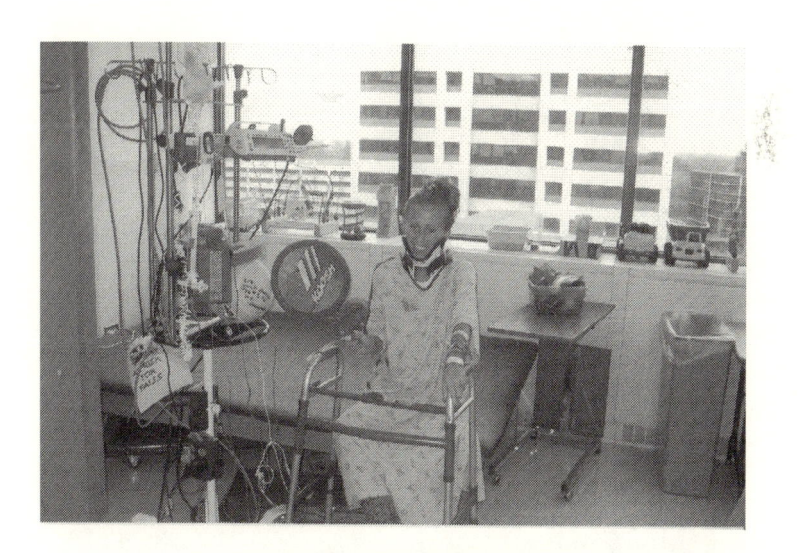

October 17, 2007 – The day before I was discharged from the hospital. As part of physical therapy, I practiced swinging a small racket—missing tennis dearly. Just like on the court, I couldn't help but shout "C'mon!" with each swing. Words cannot express the joy I felt on this day.

LIZ BURSTEN

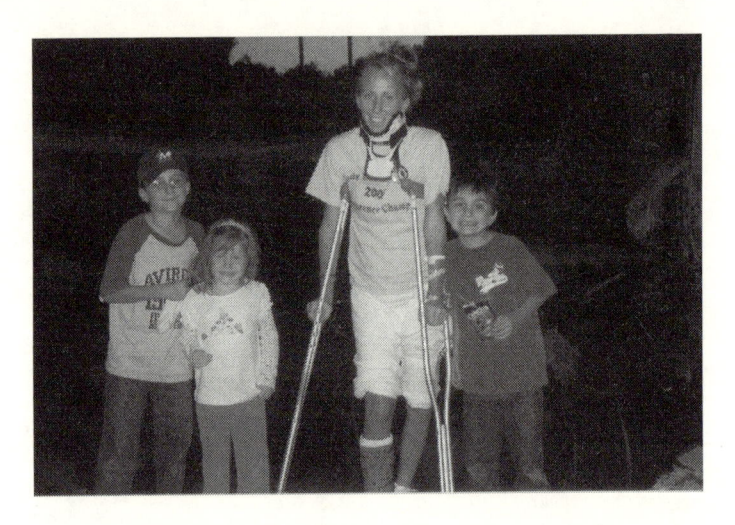

October 18, 2007 – The day I returned home from the hospital for the first time since the accident. My younger siblings waited in the driveway to welcome me back. I was overwhelmed with happiness the moment I saw their smiles. Pictured here are Christopher (Fur), Kara, and Jay.

October 18, 2007 – The day I returned home was especially meaningful as it was my little brother Jay's 8th birthday. He told me the best gift that year was having me back, and I was grateful I didn't have to miss celebrating his special day. Pictured here are my brothers Fur, Joey, Jay and my mom.

ILLUSTRATIONS

February 12, 2009 – More than a year had passed since the accident. Each birthday I celebrated after felt increasingly more meaningful, a reminder of how lucky I was to be alive. There was no place I'd rather be than surrounded by my family. Pictured here are all my siblings and my mom (with my dad behind the camera).

December 13, 2011 – Recovering from one of my many ankle surgeries, with my Papa by my side. If it hadn't been for his advice on treating my liver injury in the critical days after the accident, I may not have survived.

LIZ BURSTEN

August 28, 2012 – With my boyfriend at the time, "Spencer B." I'm forever grateful for the fateful night we met, just over a year before this photo was taken. Soulmates and best friends for life.

May 17, 2014 – Delivering the Commencement Speech at my graduation from Concordia University Wisconsin. Titled "Why Not Us?", my speech encouraged my fellow graduates to believe that we can achieve anything we set our minds to.

ILLUSTRATIONS

May 17, 2014 – Walking across the stage to receive my college diploma, filled with excitement and optimism about the future ahead.

February 25, 2016 – Bright and early, the morning of my amputation, with my mom and dad by my side. As my t-shirt read, "I can and I will." Although nervous about the road ahead, I was determined to face the challenge with optimism. I was eager for the opportunities that awaited.

75

LIZ BURSTEN

February 25, 2016 – The first moments waking up after the amputation, with my husband, Spencer, by my side. When I realized the procedure was already over, I felt an overwhelming sense of relief, hope and excitement.

March 1, 2016 – Spencer and I taking a stroll on the Oklahoma University Medical Center campus after the amputation. Soon, I would be discharged and begin the journey back home to Wisconsin.

ILLUSTRATIONS

Pictured here is "The Survivor Tree," located in the heart of Oklahoma City, a symbol of resilience after the 1995 bombing. Spencer and I visited it during the months before my amputation, when we traveled for my pre-op visit. This image hung on the wall of my bedroom in the months following the amputation, serving as a constant reminder of hope and growth.

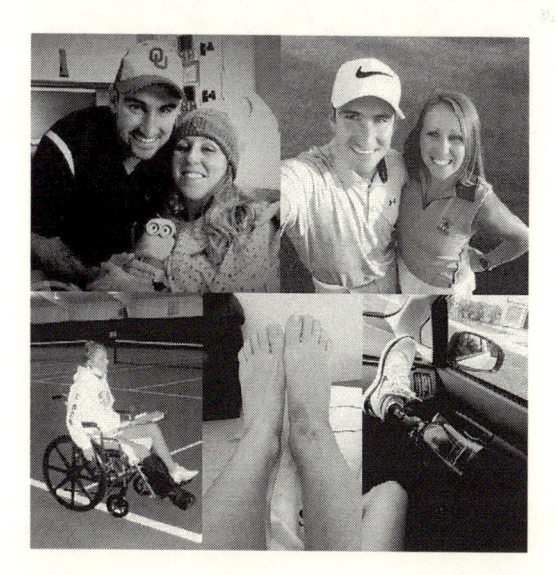

This collage represents my journey of resilience and hope, where I transformed from limited to limitless. From playing wheelchair tennis, to saying goodbye to my right foot, to walking in my first prosthetic, and even taking up golf, I am grateful for every moment and every lesson along the way.

77

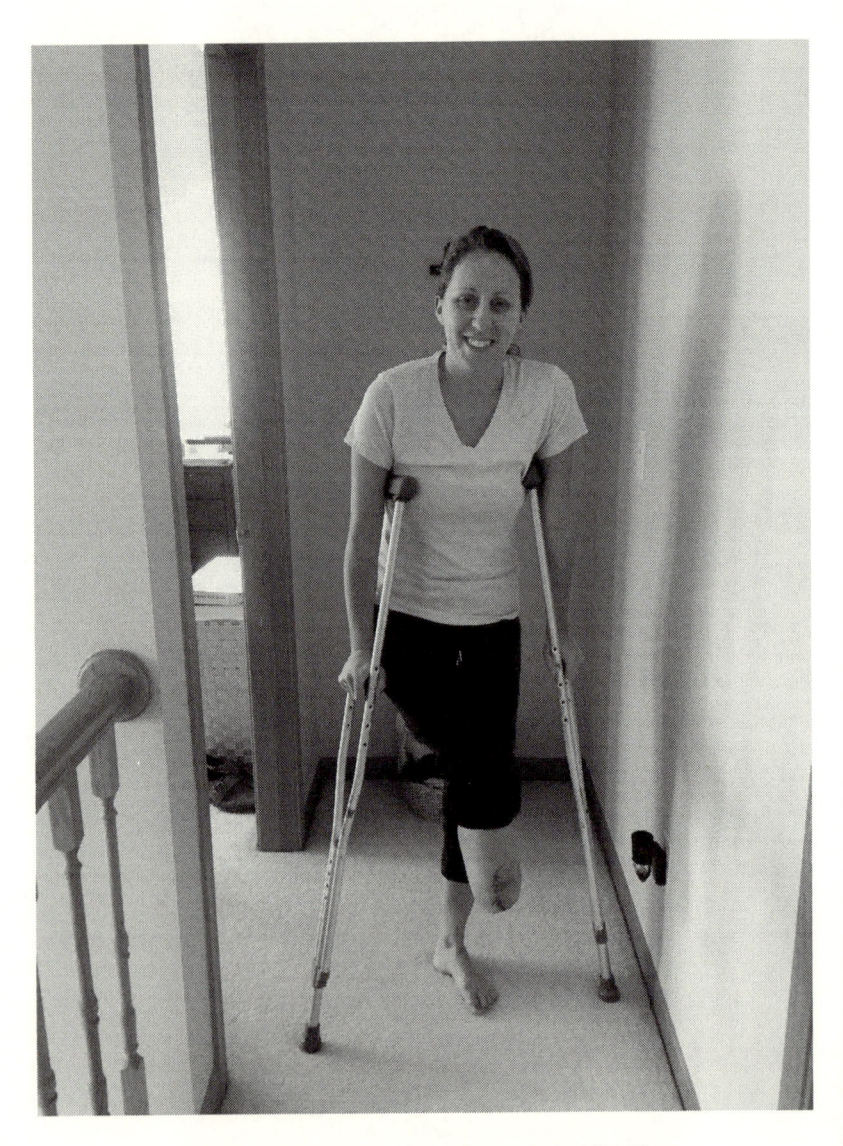

March 8, 2016 – Recovering at home. I used this time to build my mental strength while slowly working to restore my physical strength—one step at a time.

ILLUSTRATIONS

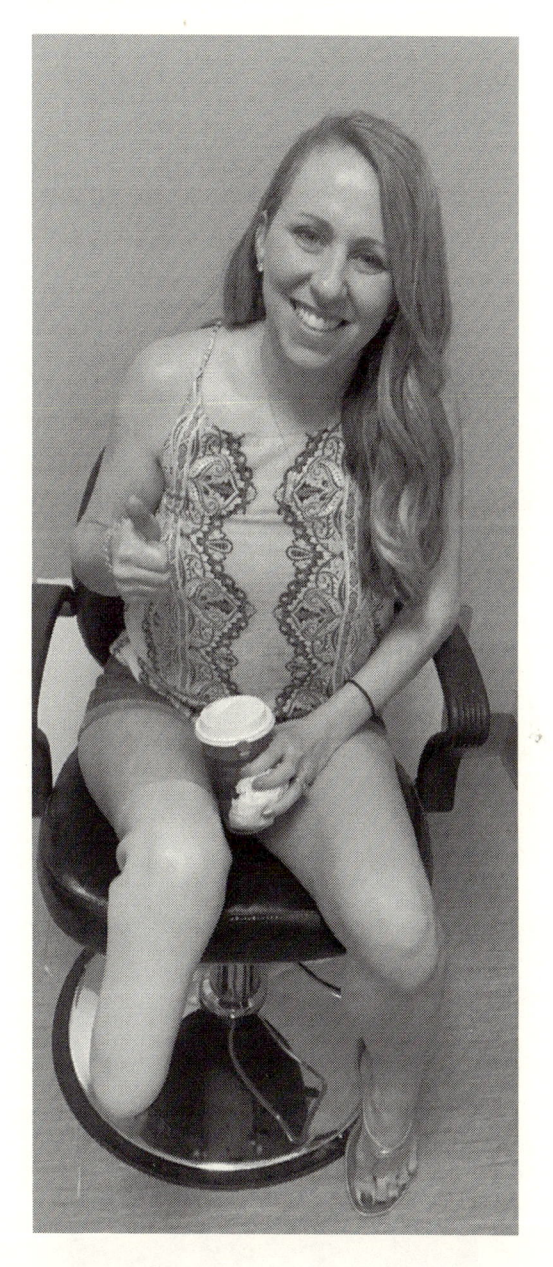

May 16, 2016 – Part 1 of my custom prosthetic complete: my first silicone liner. Just one day away from stepping into my very first prosthetic.

LIZ BURSTEN

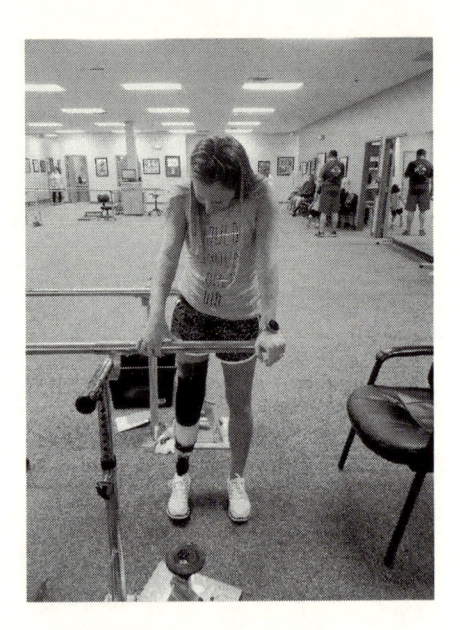

May 17, 2016 – My very first prosthetic leg. I wasn't prepared for the intense pain caused by severed nerves from the amputation, but despite it all, I was filled with excitement—knowing each day would bring progress, healing, and a step closer to being pain-free.

July 25, 2016 – Just two months into wearing my prosthetic, and I was already back on the tennis courts. Though things felt different, I was amazed by the abilities my new leg gave me.

ILLUSTRATIONS

February 25, 2017 – I earned my first gold medal in a para-athletic track meet. What made this race especially meaningful was that I ran it exactly one year after my amputation.

January 24, 2018 – My first "runway foot." This new prosthetic leg allowed me to wear high heels again—something I had long given up on and never imagined would be possible. Now my only question was, "Where's the red carpet?"

August 18, 2018 – I attended my first running clinic with the Challenged Athletes Foundation in Evanston, IL. Pictured with me is Dr. David DelToro, my Physical Medicine and Rehab doctor—the first person to help me see the world of possibilities that amputation could offer.

April 26, 2019 – After a long journey and a high-risk pregnancy, Spencer and I welcomed our son, Gordon Michael—thanks to Dr. Aida Shanti and the incredible team at the Aurora Medical Center fertility clinic in West Allis. Pictured here are one-month-old Gordon and me visiting Dr. Shanti.

ILLUSTRATIONS

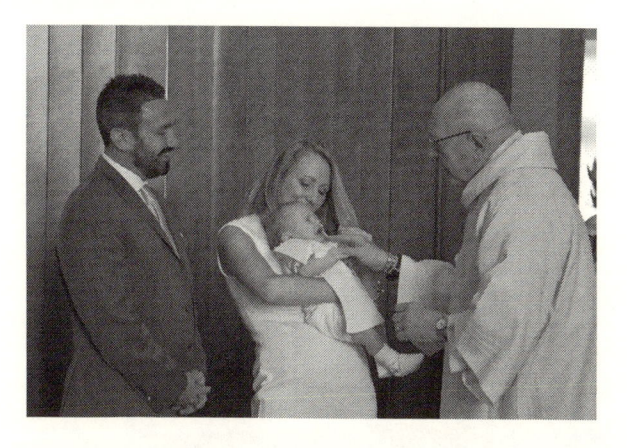

June 23, 2019 – We welcomed Gordon into the Catholic Church with a special ceremony alongside our dear Deacon Rich. Throughout my high-risk pregnancy, Deacon Rich prayed with me daily, bringing us closer to God during a challenging time. God is good!

August 12, 2019 – My first visit to Prosthetic & Orthotic Associates (POA) as a new mom, five months postpartum. I approached the challenge of balancing motherhood and life as an amputee with optimism and an open heart. Pictured with me is baby Gordon.

LIZ BURSTEN

February 19, 2021 — My first visit to POA as a mom of two, four months postpartum. My hands were full, but my heart was even fuller. Pictured with me are Gordon and baby Teddy.

July 29, 2022 — My first visit to POA as a mom of three, just two months postpartum. With three little ones to chase after, my prosthetic fittings became more frequent—I had to stay one step ahead! Pictured with me are Gordon, Teddy, and our newest addition, baby Jackson.

ILLUSTRATIONS

During our POA visit in February 2021, Spencer and I had the privilege of golfing alongside Stan Patterson, the owner and founder of POA, and Roger Underhill, my incredible prosthetist, who turns so many possibilities into reality for me.

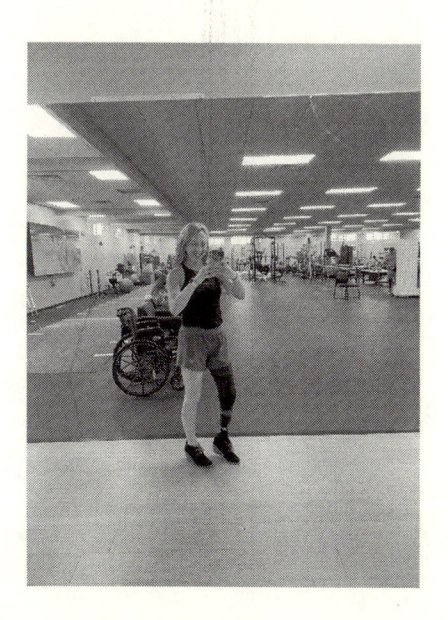

July 23, 2023 – At POA, working on my "runway foot." I'm grateful for the chance to experiment with cute and fun shoes, making fashion and function come together with my prosthetic leg.

LIZ BURSTEN

October 8, 2023, 6:17 am – Race morning in the pre-race hospitality area with Team GLASA (Great Lakes Adaptive Sports Association) before the Chicago Marathon. Spencer and I were honored to run alongside over 100 incredible teammates, having personally raised over $30,000 to support adaptive sports.

October 8, 2023, 6:48 am– GLASA's motto is "Let no one sit on the sideline." And that day, I had no intention of sitting out—I was ready to show up, give it my all, and run with purpose.

ILLUSTRATIONS

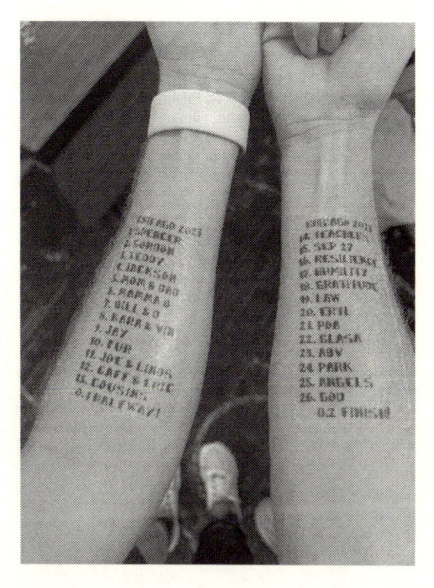

October 8, 2023, 6:59 am – Written on my arms were powerful reminders of the people, dates, and organizations that have shaped my journey—family, friends, meaningful milestones, and causes close to my heart. I ran in honor of each one, carrying their impact with me every step.

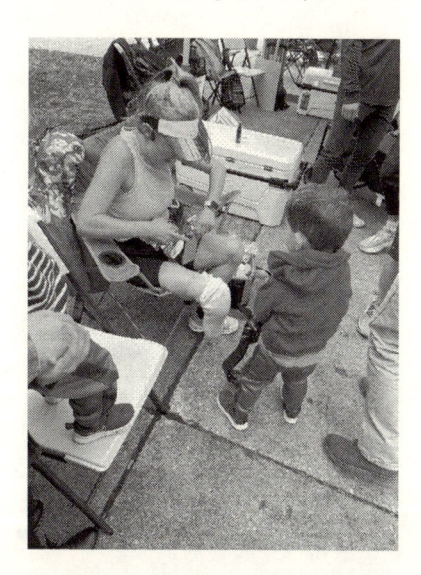

October 8, 2023, 10:43 am – My one and only "leg stop" during the Chicago Marathon—mile 15, right at Charity Mile, where our amazing family was waiting with my gear. Pictured here is Gordon proudly holding up my running blade as I swapped out silicone liners. With a quick kiss to the kids, I smiled and said, "See you in 11 miles!"

LIZ BURSTEN

October 8, 2023, 12:53 pm – Hand-in-hand, Spencer and I approached the finish line of the Chicago Marathon. After 5 hours and 35 seconds—and all the moments, miles, and memories leading up to it—WE DID IT!

October 8, 2023, 1:31 pm – A proud post-marathon moment with the whole family. Spencer and I proudly wore our medals with gratitude, surrounded by our kids whose smiles and hugs brought the perfect celebration to the finish line.

ILLUSTRATIONS

October 8, 2023, 1:34 pm – Our "village" and cheering squad on marathon day. This moment was made even sweeter with them by our side, cheering us on every step of the way. Pictured here are Eric and Catherine (cousin), Jay (brother), Teddy, myself, Spencer, Gordon, Mama B (Spencer's mom), Fur (brother), and my mom and dad.

July 19, 2024 – One of my many visits to POA. A new prosthetic fitting for mom is always a family affair, and the kids love being part of the process. Pictured with me are Gordon, Teddy and Jackson.

89

LIZ BURSTEN

September 27, 2024 – A joyful embrace on my "life day." This picture was taken exactly 17 years after my accident. Every year, September 27th is a day of remembrance for me and my family, honoring the journey and celebrating everything that has come from it. Life is beautiful.

CHAPTER 6

A CHOICE I NEVER IMAGINED

"A positive attitude gives you power over your circumstances instead of your circumstances having power over you."
—Brian Ford

Early on in my life, I looked at obstacles or challenges like they were just happening to me and I simply had to get through them. When the accident happened, although the injuries and ailments were critical and life-threatening at times, it initially felt like an acute recovery. I assumed I would have surgery, rest, heal, repeat, and then get back to normal one day. I focused on eventually putting it all behind me.

Perhaps this was the beauty in being so young when everything happened. I was naive. I didn't have a realistic understanding that the damage, repair, and radiation alone would likely pose health risks for me later in life. When I realized that parts of my recovery were actually chronic, that is when I began to feel overwhelmed, hopeless, and defeated. In 2011, when I learned that I had the power to influence my own life just by having a positive attitude, I started searching for opportunities to improve my quality of life. There was one monumental obstacle that turned into my life's greatest opportunity the years following 2011.

While I recovered tremendously from most of my injuries post-accident, it was a long and strenuous journey—mentally, spiritually, and physically. One lingering issue that continued to worsen over the years was my right ankle. At this point, my right ankle had endured ten surgeries, six pieces of hardware, and too many months of pain and non-weightbearing to count. Despite the accident and all the aftermath, I graduated from high school on time and on track. I went off to college as planned.

Years went by, and the vicious cycle of surgeries and physical therapies seemed to rotate around faster and faster each year. The years 2013 and 2014 posed incredible challenges physically, and my ankle condition was worsening as time went on. I had one of the most severe cases of post-traumatic arthritis my surgeons had ever seen. It had gotten to the point where I had to work very hard every morning just to be able to walk without my crutches or scooter.

I would first ice my ankle before getting out of bed to decrease the swelling and throbbing pain. Then I would crawl to the shower and use a chair while in the shower. If the heat from the steam wasn't enough, I'd sit on the bathroom floor with a heating pad wrapped around my ankle. This would inevitably loosen up my ankle joint, but most days I had to physically grab my right foot with both of my hands and bend my foot back and forth for the first movements. Forcing my ankle into motion caused my entire body to cringe every time.

A CHOICE I NEVER IMAGINED

From there, I just had to keep moving. If I sat down and stopped moving my ankle for even a short time, it would stiffen up all over again, which left me the option of walking with a bow-legged, sideways limp, or going through my icing and heating procedures all over again.

At this time, I was finishing up my last year of college at Concordia University of Wisconsin. I was also working full-time at a local hospital, Aurora Medical Center Grafton, as a telemetry technician in the intensive care unit (ICU). It had been my lifelong dream to become a doctor, so I was thrilled to have the opportunity to work in a hospital during my final years of undergraduate school. Sitting behind the telemetry desk opened my eyes to a whole new world of healthcare. I had much experience as a patient, but this was different. Or maybe the difference was that I was getting closer to the reality of my career. I would watch the nurses, doctors, and techs hustle back and forth past my desk all day.

For some reason, it never dawned on me until I was sitting behind that desk in the ICU that this career I was working toward was incredibly physically demanding. I felt self-conscious whenever I'd have to leave the desk for my lunch break or to use the restroom, due to my obnoxiously noticeable limp. During my lunch breaks, I thought the most about changing my career path.

One day, I walked to the vacant hospital library alone. I sat down with my head in my hands and cried. I wept as if something terrible had just happened to me, but nothing in particular happened. I was in tremendous pain and thus extremely unhappy with my quality of life. I was so uncertain about what my future would look like. In those moments, I felt hopeless.

Very quickly, my "positive attitude can change everything" voice kicked in. All of these obstacles in my life were caused by one little body part: my ankle. As I sat in the Aurora library that day, the craziest thought entered my mind: *what if I amputate?* At first, this thought seemed ridiculous. I knew nothing about amputation, and none of my doctors had ever suggested this as an option. But for some reason, it seemed like an idea worth exploring.

It took me a few weeks to speak my thought out loud. I worried my family and friends would talk me out of it. I worried my doctors would never agree to it. I worried the outcome might not actually be as great as I was imagining. Finally, I settled my worries enough to speak this idea into existence.

Naturally, the first person I mentioned this to was Spencer, and he was extremely supportive. His lack of hesitation when he encouraged me to pursue this further was all the support I needed in that moment. Just the thought of going through with this amputation idea scared me, but at the same time it excited me.

Although I didn't act upon this idea immediately, the thought of it propelled me forward in my life. I was motivated to do bigger, better things. I was forward-thinking and excited about my next chapter in life after college. During my final years of college, I picked up a business communication major. This led to the incredible opportunity of tapping into potential I didn't know was there. I began writing speeches, sharing my story, and ultimately inspiring others.

In February of 2014, I was offered the tremendous honor of being the Concordia University of Wisconsin class of 2014 commencement speaker. This opportunity gave me a chance to share my story and the learnings that came along with it, but more importantly, it drove me to dig deep within and self-reflect. Preparing for any type of graduation is a pivotal moment in one's life. It signifies the closing of one chapter and the opening of the next. As I reflected on which pieces of my story to share, I continued to contemplate the idea of amputation. I had the power to change this negative piece of my life, so why not?

Leveraging a healthy combination of my own experiences with my learnings, I crafted a powerful and influential speech to address my fellow graduates at our commencement ceremony in May. As I took the stage in my cap and gown, using one crutch to help me walk, I settled in at the podium. Before I began, I looked around the gymnasium at all the graduates, faculty, friends, and family members. I took a breath.

Luckily, I completely memorized my speech and did not feel even one bit nervous. I felt incredibly proud and thankful to be in that moment. The title of my speech was "Why not us?" The resounding message was that we (graduates) can do anything we set our minds to. I began by recognizing outstanding achievements by distinguished alumni of the university and proceeded to ask my fellow graduates, "Why not us?" and explained we, too, can achieve greatness. Next I quoted the Bible, Luke chapter twelve verse forty-eight, which says, "From everyone who has been given much, much will be demanded." As college graduates, we had been given so much and therefore much would be expected of us.

I continued to the climax of the speech, where I boldly and emotionally pronounced, "Life will inevitably throw challenges and adversity our way, but we are prepared and well-equipped to overcome anything. We can take a glass that is half empty and fill it so completely that it overflows.

We can paint that silver lining in the darkest of clouds. We can ignite that light at the end of the tunnel. Our lives are what we make them. And we have all the necessary tools to make our lives whatever we want them to be. It is up to us."

I paused for a moment as I felt my heart racing. A brief glimpse of my own life's journey popped in my mind as I continued, "Our lives can be a path of coincidence, happenstance, and luck. Or our lives can be a purposefully charted course to follow God's will, take in each moment, touch the lives of others, and make the differences that only we can make." The crowd rose to their feet as a roar of applause filled the gymnasium. And just like that, I was on to my next chapter in life!

Several long and painful months passed after sharing my wild idea of amputation with Spencer. In the summer of 2014, I was just beginning my new chapter of life. After graduating from college and moving into a new apartment, I took the first step into my career journey. My very first job post-college was as an analytical chemist at one of the world's largest biopharmaceutical companies. I started just three days after my graduation.

I loved this new part of life; I could see and feel so many opportunities that lie ahead. But my ankle continued to weigh me down. Most of my days in the lab were spent on my feet, walking from one area to another, or standing over my testing space. It became more and more challenging to keep up with while living in chronic pain.

I had an appointment with my orthopedic surgeon in June 2014, who was planning for my eleventh ankle surgery at the time. After hearing my surgeon out about his plans for my ankle, I blurted out, "Can we amputate?" It was so awkward the way I asked the question. Would he think I was crazy? He looked at me like I was crazy. There was a moment of silence.

Shortly after, he smirked and chuckled a bit. He proceeded to tell me amputation would be so much harder than what I'm currently dealing with. "You don't want to do that," he said. "That's not necessary." I could feel it in my cheeks that my face was turning bright red. I was officially embarrassed, but I was also furious. I felt dismissed and belittled. I felt that my own doctor couldn't even validate what I was going through.

So I dared to ask him another question, "Why do you think it would be harder than this?"

"You'd have to strap your leg on when you get up in the middle of the night. You wouldn't be able to just get out of bed and walk."

My eyes instantly welled up with tears. *Is he serious?* I thought to myself. I couldn't get up out of bed and walk right away now! That is when I knew amputation was the answer for me.

I didn't say anything further about the amputation to my doctor; instead, I asked what he would do instead of amputation to help me. He then explained my ten-year plan. It sounded like a business plan more than a treatment plan. This ten-year plan consisted of more surgeries, more hardware, years of pain and limitations, and loss of up to three inches in my leg due to his very special phased fusion approach. The worst part of this plan was that it would likely end with amputation as the last resort anyway.

As I sat in silence, listening to his plan, my mind wandered. I thought about the pain, swelling, medication, surgery, and physical therapy. I thought about marrying Spencer and starting a family. I wondered how my leg would hold up through pregnancy and beyond. All of these thoughts left me feeling miserable and hopeless.

And then I knew. Amputation was my only hope to escape this life filled with pain and restrictions. Now my decision changed from "To amputate or not to amputate?" to "When to amputate—at age twenty-four or thirty-four?" The answer was clear to me. My decision was made, and there was no looking back.

My surgeon's medical assistant chimed in with the most valuable piece of information in my entire amputation journey. He suggested I meet with a specific physical medicine and rehabilitation doctor, Dr. David DelToro, to learn more about what amputation could do for me. My surgeon abruptly ended the conversation and sent me off to x-ray. After my x-ray, the appointment concluded like any other. I walked out of the clinic with my paperwork in one hand and my pre-op instructions pamphlet in the other hand. Little did my surgeon know, I wasn't sold on his plan for me, and that would be the last time I stepped foot into his office, no pun intended.

That same day, I called the Froedtert Physical Medicine and Rehabilitation Clinic to schedule an appointment with Dr. DelToro. His nurse was very kind and seemed eager to help. She squeezed me into his calendar for an appointment the following week. I could not wait for this appointment, but at the same time, I was incredibly nervous. What if he agreed with my surgeon's opinion and didn't think amputation was a good option for me at this time? What if he thought I was weak? Or crazy?

Finally, the day of the appointment arrived. Immediately when Dr. DelToro entered the room, I sighed with relief, for

A CHOICE I NEVER IMAGINED

some reason. After seven long years of pain, limitations, and ultimately disability, I finally had this feeling in my gut that I would soon be free. I could truly put everything from the accident behind me. Everything.

My appointment with Dr. DelToro could not have gone better; it was the turning point I had been searching for. There are three highlights that stood out to me from this appointment. For one, Dr. DelToro absolutely validated what I was going through. Second, he absolutely agreed that amputation would give me the best quality of life, especially when compared to my surgeon's ten-year plan. Last, Dr. DelToro connected me with one of his current patients, Chris Prange Morgan, who faced the same decision as me two years prior.

After an accident that severely injured her ankle (among other things), Chris was faced with the decision to continue pursuing limb salvage or to amputate. She chose to amputate, and that opened a world of possibilities for her. I wanted nothing more than to follow in her footsteps. Chris plays a pivotal role in my story as I truly did follow in her footsteps.

We met for coffee one afternoon where she let me openly ask every single question that came to mind. She willingly shared her journey and many of her lessons learned along the way. Every detail she shared further reaffirmed my belief that amputation was the next best step for me. Chris and I continued to keep in touch after this initial meeting, and she offered support as I officially began planning for my amputation.

The most critical characters in my amputation story all came from the guidance of Chris. My surgeon, who performed the amputation, was the same one as Chris's. My trauma counselor, who examined my psychological state as I navigated through this process, was the same one as Chris's. My incredible team of prosthetists, who have given me the ability to live my life without limits, was the same team as Chris's. I owe much of my success post-amputation to Chris. I will be forever grateful for the light she has shed on my path.

When I made the connection with the surgeon Chris used for her amputation, I felt even more confident that amputation was the right choice for me. One thing after the next continued to fall into place. However, when this piece of the puzzle was in place, I felt even more strong and confident in my decision. As I mentioned in chapter 2, Dr. William Ertl performed my amputation at the Oklahoma University Hospital in Oklahoma City.

Since I was planning for my own amputation in advance, I had the luxury of time. Spencer and I flew down to Oklahoma City to meet Dr. Ertl six months prior to the amputation. Thankfully, Dr. Ertl agreed with my proposal to amputate and advised that he would have recommended that for me at least three surgeries ago. He explained to me that my last three surgeries caused far more damage than improvement. Each surgery attempted variations of revascularization to my talus (ankle bone), including the bone graft taken from my own tibia and implanted into my talus. Each of those three surgeries left larger deficits in my talus, which was never successfully revascularized.

In that very first appointment with Dr. Ertl, he gave me hope. He shared stories of what he has seen in his experience with amputees. I couldn't wait to be one of the stories he would tell other patients about. He assured me that my life as an amputee would be superior to anything further ankle surgeries could do for me. He was so confident but also compassionate. He talked through both scenarios for me, the option to amputate versus continuing the limb salvage. He validated my feelings and then some. He was empathetic and saw me as a whole person, not just an ankle to work on.

During our one-hour visit, Dr. Ertl also took the time to walk me through his surgical plan. We talked about what kinds of activities I like to do, which would determine the types of prosthesis I would need. He precisely measured the exact amount of my leg to be amputated to ensure I would have a specific prosthetic setup. I knew nothing about the prosthetic world at that time.

The amount of my leg that he wanted to amputate made it so that my everyday prosthetic leg would not require a pylon component, just a socket and a foot. The pylon component is a metal pole which is typically used to connect the socket and the foot while giving the leg the appropriate heigh – and I wouldn't need that piece. A prosthetic setup without this component means the foot connects directly to the socket. This setup is incredible and allows for so much balance, comfort, strength, and stability on my amputated side.

After we completed discussing the surgical plan, I had one question. "When can I schedule the surgery?" And the rest is history.

The opportunity to meet with Dr. Ertl was clearly the highlight of the trip, but there was one more highlight. Since our flight back home wasn't until the next day, Spencer and I had some free time while in Oklahoma City. We decided to visit the Oklahoma City National Museum. This museum takes you through the story of the 1995 Oklahoma City bombing and the community's inspiring response to it.

LIZ BURSTEN

After walking through the museum, you are taken through the beautiful, inspirational outdoor memorial. This memorial includes a field of empty chairs, representing all 168 lives lost on that fateful day. There is also a memorial wall, a reflective pool, and a symbolic structure of gates. All of these elements rest on the footprint of what used to be a federal building prior to the bombing.

One part of this memorial instantly overwhelmed me with emotion. Emotions of hope, optimism, and awe consumed me. At the center of the outdoor memorial space is a tree. This tree is known as the Survivor Tree. It is an American Elm, which bore witness to the violence of April 19, 1995, and withstood the full force of the attack. After the bombing occurred, the community came together to care for the tree, nursing it back to life. Almost thirty years later, it continues to stand as a living symbol of resilience.

Spencer and I stood in front of the tree for several minutes. As I observed its beauty along every intricate branch and leaf, I settled in with the thought that I would soon be losing a limb. It made me feel sad. Then my feeling quickly shifted to hope as I thought about the Oklahoma City community. They must have felt much sorrow and pain, living through the aftermath of the bombing. However, as a community, they came together and created this beautiful icon of hope and resilience, which will continue to inspire its visitors for years to come.

When I first thought of amputation, it seemed scary and extreme. Amputating my leg and knowing it was my choice to do so was undoubtedly one of my life's greatest obstacles. But it led to the most incredible opportunities. See past the obstacles. No matter what, there is always an opportunity.

A CHOICE I NEVER IMAGINED

EXERCISE: Obstacles to Opportunities[8]

Create a listing of current obstacles you are facing. Circle which ones are within your control. Rewrite and rephrase each obstacle as an opportunity.

Obstacles to Opportunites	Date:
Current Obstacle	**Rephrase as an Opportunity**
Example: I have extreme pain when walking.	Example: I am alive. I can find a new way to move around without pain
1	1
2	2
3	3
4	4
5	5
6	6
7	7

---

[8] Denice Hinden, "How to Turn Any Obstacles Into Opportunities In 6 Steps," LinkedIn.com, November 11, 2023, https://www.linkedin.com/pulse/how-turn-any-obstacles-opportunities-6-steps-denice-hinden-lk5oc/.

8	
9	
10	

8	
9	
10	

I am thankful to have had the opportunity to have courageous conversations with my surgeon, through which I took my treatment plan into my own hands. I am thankful to have had the opportunity of meeting Dr. DelToro. I am thankful to have met Chris and dared to explore the unknown. I am thankful to have had the opportunity to take a chance, flying down to meet the surgeon who would perform my amputation in Oklahoma City.

All these opportunities could have easily been foreseen as obstacles, but not for me. This collection of life encounters has molded into the most fulfilling opportunity to live the life of my dreams—A LIFE WITHOUT LIMITS!

CHAPTER 7

WHEN LETTING GO MEANS LIVING

"Show up in every single moment like you're meant to be there."
—Marie Forleo

As I shared in chapter 2, from the very first moment waking up after the amputation, I felt an immediate weight lifted off my shoulders. In that very first moment, I felt with every fiber of my being that I made the right decision. In fact, every moment from then on was much easier than I anticipated. There was a new level of excitement in the air.

A whole new world of possibilities had just opened up. More than ever before, I was ecstatic about the recovery period. I didn't know exactly what was on the other side of that recovery, but I knew it would be significantly better than the life I had been living between the accident and the amputation. I was ready, mentally and physically, to transform my life from limited to limitless.

After three short months of a smooth and peaceful recovery, Spencer and I were on a plane down to Orlando, Florida, to have my first prosthetic made. This was the step in my journey I had been looking forward to the most! Orlando is home to the absolute best prosthetic facility in the world, Prosthetic & Orthotic Associates, fondly referred to as POA. Remember one of the most critical characters in my amputation story, Chris? She introduced me to this remarkable place. I wasn't kidding when I said I followed in her footsteps. From my medical team all the way to my prosthetist and even the components and suspension of my prosthetic—all exactly the same as Chris.

I'm often asked why I journey all the way to Orlando for my prosthetic care. Whenever I have the opportunity to share my why, it often leads to someone connecting me with a fellow amputee, and I point them in the direction of POA. A few words I would use to describe POA are life-changing, transformative, inspiring, and limitless. Words, however, cannot do this exceptional place justice. POA is one of the most special places I have ever encountered. POA is a place where dreams come true, doubts are shattered, and possibilities are endless. This is why we chose to journey such a long way for my prosthetic care.

I arrived at POA in May 2016 for my first prosthetic fitting on a Sunday evening. I entered through the front door and crutched down a long hallway to meet my prosthetist. As I took my time crutching down the hall, I couldn't help but notice the pictures hanging on the walls. All around the entire facility at POA are large, framed pictures of amputees doing remarkable things.

WHEN LETTING GO MEANS LIVING

The pictures showcased a wide variety of lower extremity amputees in all shapes and sizes: from below-knee to bilateral to above-knee amputees. And all different kinds of people: from Paralympic athletes to war veterans to children. They were all warriors and survivors in their own way. They were all patients of POA. Now my level of excitement for this step in the journey was through the roof. I couldn't wait to begin.

The first two days of the process consisted of fittings and measurements. POA has their own manufacturing facility on site, where they custom-make several components of the prosthetic. On day three, it was planned that I'd step into my very first prosthetic for the very first time.

It was Tuesday morning as I arrived at my appointment. I sat down in a chair and waited for my prosthetist to bring out my brand new, custom-made leg socket.

As I waited, I chatted with other patients. POA has a unique setup. It's not your typical medical clinic arrangement where you sit in a waiting room and get called back to a private exam room for your appointment. At POA, you let yourself in the front door and walk yourself back to the 7,000-square-foot open space where the walls are lined with chairs and couches and the center is filled with walking bars and various prosthetic tools and supplies. In the back of this open space is a private gym, and there is even a miniature turf running track on the side. In total, POA's facility is 22,000 square feet, which includes their very own manufacturing and product fabrication laboratory on site.

On the day I learned to walk with a prosthetic, the room was filled with inspiration. One fellow amputee was in town to tune up her running blade prior to her upcoming Paralympic track meet. Another was a frequent user of his wheelchair, working on spending more time in his prosthetics and less time in his chair. Another was a young girl, getting her first ever running blade, which helped her run and bounce around just like any other kid.

Each of us amputees had a different journey, but we shared in the common goal to shatter the limitations our disabled bodies caused us. We all had a story: from car wrecks and cancers to shark attacks and lawn-mowing accidents to diabetes and genetic deficiencies. Each of our stories were different, but we all had a purpose, something we were working toward. And POA was helping each of us achieve our goals, one step at a time.

Acclimating to my very first prosthetic was no walk in the park, no pun intended. I wasn't prepared for the pain I would feel during the desensitizing process. In a below-knee amputation, five major nerve endings are severed. Post-amputation, those nerve endings must go through the process of desensitizing. The only way to accomplish this is to touch and stimulate the area of the body where those nerve endings are buried. After three months of elevation and rest to my limb, those nerve endings were hardly touched or stimulated.

When I slipped my limb into my prosthetic socket for the first time, I felt every little nerve firing, burning, and stinging. The site of my incision felt like a deep bruise, pulsing and throbbing. The pain was strong, but I was stronger. Every bit of pain and suffering since the accident has conditioned me to overcome this. I was determined to get through this, to remain strong and to keep focused on the light at the end of the tunnel: my life without limits. Although the process was challenging, the fittings went perfectly. And just eight short days after I arrived at POA, I was on a plane heading back home.

My main goal was to wear my prosthetic from the moment I woke up in the morning until the moment I went to bed at the end of the night. In order to get there, I had to break it down into smaller goals. I had to be patient but persistent. During my first weeks home with my new prosthetic, I set daily goals for adapting to my prosthetic. This began with things like wearing my leg for thirty minutes on and thirty minutes off.

Whether sitting or standing, just wearing my leg helped me acclimate. I also incorporated walking goals into my days. I started with just walking down my driveway and touching the mailbox. The next day I would walk to the street and past my next-door neighbor's house and then back. This quickly turned into me walking down the block and eventually walking up to two miles at a time. It took me about six weeks of practice to get to that point.

I visited POA for new fittings four times during my first year. Each time, I'd walk away with more comfort and more abilities. Very quickly, I became a pro in my walking leg. I achieved my goal of wearing my prosthetic every waking hour of each day. I no longer limited the number of times I'd go between the upper and lower levels of my house. I stopped paying attention to how much time I was standing on my feet. I hadn't used an icepack in months. I'd even played tennis again!

Day by day, the limitations I once had were fading away. In October 2016, eight months post-amputation, I was fitted for my first ever running blade. After the accident, I accepted that I would never play competitive sports again, let alone run. But part of my rehab post-amputation included specific exercises to prepare to run one day. Those exercises felt so tiny and insignificant, but I was astounded when I strapped on my blade and ran for the first time. My form was nearly perfect. It felt so right. This was a long-awaited milestone that I couldn't believe I was accomplishing less than a year after the amputation.

Eager to put my running blade to good use, I joined an adaptive sports group when I returned home—Great Lakes Adaptive Sports Association (GLASA). Since I loved my new ability to run, I joined the track and field team and started competing in the hundred-meter and two-hundred-meter races. The feeling of being able to run competitively was incredible. I will never forget the track meet on my one-year ampuversary, February 25, 2017. I placed first in the division of female below-knee amputees. I even finished my two-hundred-meter ahead of three able-bodied runners in the race. I couldn't believe it.

That day, when I stood on the podium to receive my medal, I knew I was called to something big. Running that race on that day was the most liberating feeling. I was empowered. I was strong. I was free—free from pain, free from disability, free from limitation. I finally achieved a long-awaited milestone. It happened! I was living my life without limits. The ambitious voice inside of me began to wonder what possibilities I could achieve next.

Even more than the satisfaction of running and being a competitor again, the ordinary moments were perhaps more rewarding. One year into amputation, I was successfully wearing my prosthetic all day, every day. From the moment I got out of the shower each morning until the moment I snuggled up in my bed at night, I wore my prosthetic. It became part of me.

In the year leading up to the amputation, I worried if I'd feel confident or beautiful again. And I did! I felt more confident than I ever had in my life. It is evident that my first year post-amputation was physically transformational, but the mental transformation was so much greater. More than ever, I truly believed anything was possible. And that is a beautiful thing. Often, we place our own limitations on ourselves. It's all in our heads.

Will you believe in yourself? Or do you doubt yourself? Are you criticizing yourself? Or cheering yourself on? The choice is yours.

EXERCISE: Shatter Self-Imposed Limits[9]

Journal to the below prompts and put these thoughts into *action*!

1. Expose Your Limiting Beliefs
   - Write down beliefs you have about yourself or your life that are limiting you from reaching your full potential. If you are having a hard time with this, feel free to ask a close friend or family member to help you dig deep. (e.g., "I was injured in a car accident and now I am living with chronic pain. I will never be fulfilled in life because I can't do the things I used to be able to do.")
2. Reframe Your Perspective
   - Take each limiting belief and rewrite it as a "limitless belief." (e.g., "I am alive and here for a reason. With the right mental attitude, I can build a beautiful life. I can choose to enjoy the excitement of finding new dreams to pursue.")
3. Act as If Your Limitless Belief Were True
   - Write down specific actions you can take to begin putting your new limitless belief into practice. Be realistic. Consider what fits into your life *today*! (e.g., "I can amputate my leg. I can work really hard to adapt to life as an amputee. I can run a marathon. I can share my journey to inspire and help others.")

---

[9] Nader, "Breaking Free: How To Identify And Overcome Your Limiting Beliefs," Inner Light Journal, innerlightjournal.com, February 25, 2024, https://innerlightjournal.com/overcome-your-limiting-beliefs/#:~:text=This%20guide%20is%20dedicated%20to%20unraveling%20the%20complex,for%20those%20who%20seek%20to%20redefine%20their%20lives.

4. Create Accountability
    - Share your responses to the first three questions with a close friend or family member. Consider this person your accountability partner. Sometimes just sharing what you are working toward with one person is enough to move the needle forward!
5. Unleash Your Life Without Limits
    - Be mindful of your success. Each time you recognize a behavior or action you are taking to shatter the limits you previously placed on yourself, write it down and celebrate it! Continue the momentum and continue to repeat this exercise as much as needed.

It's no surprise that things will happen to us that we cannot control. Perhaps we will encounter limitations from the world, or even from our own bodies when illness or injury are upon us. Despite this fact, we can still have a limitless lifestyle. When we shatter limitations in our mind, we put ourselves into a constant state of finding the window when the door closes. Remember, you are capable of exactly what you tell yourself. Your potential is whatever you tell yourself it is. Even when things are out of our control, there is so much that we can control just within our own minds.

CHAPTER 8

HOPE AGAINST THE ODDS

"Press forward. Do not stop. Do not linger in your journey, but strive for the mark set before you."
—George Whitefield

Right off the bat, post-amputation, the limitless lifestyle I'd dreamed of became my reality. As soon as my new normal actually felt normal to me, the next bump in the road came along.

In February of 2017, I was twenty-six years old and living my best life. My career was moving forward, I was enjoying married life and loving every minute of working toward physical goals with my track and field endeavors. Life was good. I was reaching for the stars and then some. But I was falling short in one area – I couldn't get pregnant.

After nearly two years of trying for pregnancy, I sought medical attention to understand the challenges I was facing. After some months of trial-and-error treatments and various diagnostic tests, I was told that I had a very low probability of successfully conceiving and carrying a pregnancy. The most extreme diagnostic technique was a series of exploratory surgeries, a laparoscopy was first.

My doctor shared the preliminary results with me immediately following the procedure. The images he showed me looked like thick spiderwebs inside my body. I had massive amounts of scar tissue encasing all my reproductive organs, as well as most of my other abdominal organs. Both of my ovaries and my fallopian tubes were completely covered in scar tissue. After reviewing my medical chart, my doctor explained to me that this scarring likely occurred after my accident when my liver tore and the bile filled my entire abdomen.

Clearly my reproductive organs weren't operating the way they should have been, but I was surprised that my other abdominal organs had been functioning for all those years post-accident. It looked awful! In the laparoscopy, my doctor removed all the scar tissue that was accessible. However, he explained to me that more scar tissue would form from what he did, but it wouldn't be nearly as much as the amount he removed.

Now that my reproductive organs were "free," I was instructed to try to conceive for three more months. If I was unsuccessful at that time, we would pursue the next steps. Can you guess what happened? Nothing. And three months later I underwent an exploratory hysteroscopy, which revealed several large fibroids inside my uterus. At this point, my doctor was certain that conceiving naturally was nearly impossible. I felt defeated, ashamed, miserable, and confused.

My whole entire life I dreamt of being a mom. And now that may not be an option for me? After all I've been through, are you kidding me? Sure, I was strong, healthy, and alive. But I felt so empty inside when the thought of not having children came to mind. Prior to receiving this news, I felt on top of the world. I had endured every challenge from both the accident and the amputation, and I came out on top. Suddenly it felt like none of that mattered.

I've said it before and I'll say it again: each challenge I've encountered truly made me stronger in the end. So by this time, I had incredible mental strength. After the initial feelings of sadness sunk in, I was strong enough to let the feelings of hope and pride rise to the surface. I was reaching and exceeding my potential in so many ways, but this was an area where my potential evolved in a negative way.

Lying in bed one night shortly after receiving this news, I remember thinking to myself, *It's okay, meet yourself where you are. You are here.* I fell asleep that night repeating that phrase in my head, like a mantra. In my head I eventually shortened the mantra. I fell asleep that night thinking to myself over and over, *You are here, you are here, you are here . . .* until I drifted off to sleep.

The very next day, I woke up feeling better about my situation. I still had that mantra from the night before sounding loud and proud in my mind. The moment I focused on exactly where I was, I stopped hanging on to what could have been or what should have been. I stopped stressing over losing a critical piece of my dream and started focusing on where I was, which led to what came next.

On that very day, I took action. Action #1: I began researching how to go about adopting a baby. Right away, I filled out two applications to two different agencies for domestic adoptions. The next step was to wait for a call from the agencies for an orientation prior to adding us to the waitlists. Action #2: My doctor recommended I set up a consultation with a fertility specialist, so I did. When I met with the fertility specialist, she aligned with my doctor's prognosis, which felt discouraging all over again. But then she proceeded to share with me my options. From there, Spencer and I made our decision and came up with a plan.

Feeling my potential to become a mother slip through my fingers was an absolutely emotional and painful experience. I could have sat and cried about that for days. I could have felt sorry for myself. I could have mourned the loss of the pieces of my life the accident continued to take from me. I could have frozen, but I didn't. Instead, I forged a path forward. I endeavored on a beautiful new journey to change my potential, or at least try to.

Every step of my journey to becoming a mother was uncertain. Most of the time, I doubted it would work out. But there is something to be said about trying, giving it all you've got. I had to try. I couldn't give up. And guess what? After just four months of fertility treatments, it happened. I was pregnant!

All along, Spencer and I were preparing for the worst but hoping for the best. Anyone who has gone through fertility treatments knows that you never really feel like you're out of the woods. From the restrictions the doctors gave me to the warnings of things to look out for terrified me. I was a nervous wreck for the first trimester. When I finally made it through the first trimester, I felt more confident, which is common even for natural pregnancies. Things were progressing, and everything seemed to be going as planned.

Finally, the day arrived for my twenty-week anatomy scan of the baby. I couldn't wait! Everything went great, or so I thought. About an hour after my appointment, my doctor called me. He urged me to immediately stop what I was doing, go home, lie in bed, and stay there as much as possible. I was diagnosed with an insufficient cervix and was already beginning to dilate.

The doctor recommended modified bedrest, which meant lying in bed, or in a reclined position, as much as possible. I could still shower, make myself meals, and of course use the restroom. But other than that, I was to stay in bed. This was a familiar feeling to me, going from finally feeling confident and strong to nervous and helpless. I began with pep talks to myself right away, but it didn't help. Of course, Spencer was the greatest support in the world, but I still couldn't help but worry. My anxiety was through the roof, which could not have been good for the baby. The mantra kicked in again. I thought, *It's okay. Meet yourself where you are. You are here.*

I learned twenty-four weeks is the earliest the baby is considered viable and has a chance to survive. Going from twenty weeks pregnant to twenty-four weeks felt like a lifetime. Then when we hit the twenty-four-week milestone, we were simply taking it one week at a time, just hoping to maintain the pregnancy as long as possible. My mantras and mental strength only took me so far. I had never felt worry and anxiety like this in my life. It was at this time that the most remarkable blessing landed on my doorstep—literally.

God works in wonderfully mysterious ways. I am a firm believer that everything happens for a reason. What comes next was definitely God's work. Before Spencer and I were married, we went through marriage preparation classes at our parish. The deacon at our church, Deacon Rich, was our instructor. But he was so much more than that; he became our mentor, role model, and friend.

When Deacon Rich heard the news that I was on bedrest due to my high-risk pregnancy, he showed up on our doorstep. Spencer was gone at work, but of course I was home in bed. I went downstairs to answer the door. Through the window I saw Deacon standing there with a smile on his face and a Bible in his hand. He asked if he could come in and pray with me and I welcomed him in. I shared with Deacon exactly what we were going through. I told him about my worries and fears. With the jolliest, most poised and assured sound in his voice, Deacon said, "Ah, you don't have to do that [worry]. God will take care of it. Everything is in God's hands."

Tears filled my eyes, and a sense of calm filled my heart. This was yet again a turning point for me and a huge life lesson. From that moment on, when I felt any sort of anxiety or worries, I turned to prayer. I reminded myself of Deacon's life-changing words on that day. Deacon Rich continued to visit me at home nearly every day. He began bringing the Eucharist to me and giving special blessings to the baby. This was an extraordinary evolution in my potential. After years of working on my mental strength, I had lost the deep connection I had with faith. Now it all came back together. In the face of hardship, my mental strength paired with my faith and reliance on the Lord gave me the ability to get through even the most challenging of circumstances.

In the end, my lifelong dream of becoming a mother came true. Spencer and I became parents to our beautiful baby boy, our miracle, Gordon Michael Bursten, on March 9, 2019. I made it all the way to thirty-five and a half weeks in my pregnancy, which was unbelievable.

Shortly after the birth of Gordon, we encountered another miracle. On Gordon's first birthday, we announced to our friends and family that we were expecting another baby! The most amazing part about this pregnancy was that it all happened on our own, no fertility treatments necessary.

My potential continued to evolve. After a long (full-term) and healthy pregnancy, Theodore (Teddy) James Bursten was born on October 3, 2020.

Believe it or not, one more miracle came along the following year. On Teddy's first birthday, we announced to our friends and family that we were expecting our third baby. We couldn't believe it! Once again, it happened all on our own. It was truly a miracle. Jackson Thomas Bursten was born on May 11, 2022.

EXERCISE: Realizing Potential[10]

Journal to the prompts below. Reflect on your responses in times of hardship. Repeat and expand this exercise as much as needed!

As you strive to reach your full potential, keep this mantra in mind: "Every day in every way I am getting better and better!"

Realizing Potential	Date:

Step 1: Assess Your Strenghts

Do you know what you are really good at? What has always been easy for you?

Step 2: Assess Your Weaknesses

What do you struggle with? When do you feel out of your comfort zone?

Step 3: Think about What You Like

What do you enjoy doing? Who do you enjoy being with? What parts of your life are your favorite?

---

[10] "8 Steps to Realizing Your Full Potential," Warrior Mind Coach, warriormindcoach.com, September 22, 2021, https://warriormindcoach.com/8-steps-to-realizing-your-full-potential.

> **Step 4: Think about What You Want to Accomplish**
>
> What do you want to do? What fulfills you?

> **Step 5: Avoid Distractions**
>
> What/who could possibly interfere with you reaching your full potential? Can you think of steps to take to minimize these distractions?

> **Step 6: Find a Mentor**
>
> Who in your life will hold you accountable and encourage you?

> **Step 7: Make a Commitment**
>
> What steps can you take to make a conscious decision to accomplish what you have defined in step four?

Life is ever-changing and nothing lasts forever. In the last seventeen years, there have been several occurrences where I haven't been able to establish a consistent "normal" in my life. Right when I'd adapt to the latest and greatest change in my life, a curve ball would come along. I've learned over time that you will find peace and power when you realize where you are and accept it when changes and challenges happen in life.

CHAPTER 9

CHASING THE CHALLENGE

"You can often change your circumstances by changing your attitude."
—Eleanor Roosevelt

Speaking from experience, attitude can certainly change circumstances. In November of 2022, my family and I traveled to Denver, Colorado, to spend Thanksgiving with Spencer's brother, Tyler, and his family for Thanksgiving. Together with Tyler's wife, Sarah, and their two children, Penelope and Charles, we enjoyed the holiday weekend. Earlier that month, Sarah completed her first marathon, the New York City Marathon. I was amazed and inspired as she shared her experience with us. This was when the first thought popped into my head about running a marathon.

A few days went by after we returned home to Wisconsin. Spencer and I were getting ready for bed when he mentioned that he and Tyler decided they wanted to run a marathon together.

My heart pounded rapidly in my chest. Then I said it. Right then and there, out loud, I told Spencer that I was thinking about running a marathon too.

I shamelessly stole the thunder and interrupted Spencer's own excitement about his decision to run a marathon for the first time. (Sorry, Spence.) This was a huge deal and a big decision that Spencer just made too! As the words left my mouth, I wanted them back. Aside from wishing that I let Spencer have his moment before making it about me right away, I was questioning and doubting myself.

Then Spencer responded. Of course, he was encouraging and supportive as usual. But at first, he asked me if I was serious. I acknowledged I'd have to see my doctor and a physical therapist to explore if this were truly an option, but ultimately I told him I was definitely serious about this.

Spencer held out his hand for a high five then pulled me in for a hug. We looked each other in the eyes and agreed, right then and there, we were going to run the Chicago Marathon 2023 together. Spencer turned off the lights, and we went to sleep. Well, Spencer did. I lay there awake for most of the night, playing through all the possible scenarios in my head. I was determined to figure out a way to achieve this goal.

The next day, I booked a consultation appointment with a trainer who worked closely with amputees at Froedtert's Physical Medicine and Rehabilitation Clinic. I knew running a marathon would be an uphill battle, especially since I had never run more than a 5K before. I also hadn't been consistently running since 2021, and for a good reason too. In August of 2021, I had a revision surgery to my amputated limb. The purpose of this surgery was twofold. Motive number one was to remove the atrophied muscle and tissue,

CHASING THE CHALLENGE

which caused complications with my prosthetic fit. These complications resulted in frequent, incredibly painful sores.

Motive number two of the surgery, most importantly, was to secure and repurpose the nerve endings that were severed in the amputation. The surgery took my severed nerves and tied them into my quad muscles, a procedure referred to as targeted muscle reinnervation (TMR). This surgical intervention was intended to minimize the debilitating phantom limb pain I had been experiencing in the years following my amputation. Both parts of the surgery were successful.

Between recovering from the surgery and recovering from pregnancy, all while working full-time and keeping up with two toddlers and a newborn, running moved down on my priority list. I remember in July of 2022 I tried to run for the first time since the revision surgery. My right leg and lower back were trembling and twitching. In that moment I realized I should probably undergo some sort of physical therapy before just going for a run.

After all, the surgery did leave me with an eight-inch scar straight down the center of my hamstrings. My thigh muscles underwent severe trauma, and I never took the time to care for them properly due to the sudden pregnancy. And here I was, four months later making the decision to run a marathon in eleven months. I was going to need all the help I could get, so I started right away.

It was early December when I first met with my new trainer at the rehab clinic. My first few visits consisted of stretching and mobility exercises. Until finally one day, I was instructed to bring my running blade so we could begin training on the tread. The first training session on the tread was underwhelming, to say the least. I ran for only five minutes at a very slow speed before my right quad, hamstrings, and lower back began to tremble and twitch. It was exactly what happened last time I attempted to run in July.

My trainer advised me to run for just five minutes every other day, adding one minute to my run every other time I ran. This meant that twice per week, I would add an extra minute to my run. By the time I saw my trainer the following week, I was up to seven minutes and still felt the same. But I stuck with it. Slowly but surely the trembling and shaking stopped. In addition to my running regimen, I was also religiously working on the stretches and mobility exercises. These initial workouts were so tiny and felt insignificant in the moment, but I had to start somewhere. Three weeks later, I went in for a regular visit with my trainer. At this time, I was running just fifteen minutes at a time and felt ready to get to the next level in my training.

When I excitedly asked about adding more to my training regimen, my trainer responded in the most discouraging way possible. The words he said stuck with me to this day. He said he wouldn't recommend going "from couch to marathon" within this timeframe for any normal, healthy person. And then he proceeded to say, "Especially for you." Not only did he classify me as someone who was not normal and healthy, he also didn't believe in me.

From a health perspective, I was certainly healthy. In fact, as an amputee, to register for the marathon, I had to provide medical clearance from my doctor, which I did. From a "normal" perspective, is anybody normal? And when my trainer said he wouldn't recommend this journey "especially for me," I realized that he didn't know me at all. He looked at me like I was less than the average person, just because of my physical challenges. The reality was, I am more than the average person due to my unwavering resilience and determination. I was in shock with my trainer's advice. I went through the motions and finished the appointment, then I never returned to that trainer again.

Although the experience with my trainer was far from ideal, I am thankful for the foundational elements he taught me. The stretching and mobility exercises carried me through my entire season of training. But as for the running regimen, I took the next steps into my own hands. I created my own training plan, a combination between the Hal Higdon and Nike training plans. Of course, I significantly modified it and was only running four days per week due to extended rest required on my amputated leg. I used stationary biking as my cross-training for most of the time. At times, my training felt like a roller coaster, and I had to change course several times.

The experience of training granted me the opportunity to exercise patience in a way I never had before. It was a balancing act. Not only did I have to get my endurance and strength to a certain level to run the marathon, but I was so careful not to overdo it. I didn't want to require too much rest or downtime. Throughout my ten months of training for the marathon, I was determined to still show up for my kids the same way I would if I wasn't pursuing such an ambitious feat. I must admit, there were times where I had to take no-leg days due to swelling and skin irritation after long runs. I wasn't proud of that. After happening a few times, I tried my best not to push myself too much so that I could still wear my leg all day every day to take care of my kids.

Although training was hard work, I loved every bit of it and always looked forward to it. Each time I strapped on my running blade and tied up my running shoe, I felt immensely grateful. The feeling never got old.

Due to our busy schedules with work and caring for the kids, Spencer and I did most of our training separately. But every now and then, we would schedule a date and go on a long run together. This was so much fun! One of our favorite routes to run together was in our soon-to-be hometown, Cedarburg. During the months leading up to the marathon, our dream home was in the making and we loved taking weekend trips to check it out. Spencer's mom, Mama B, lives in Cedarburg, so going to see our new house always gave us an excuse to stop for a visit.

On a warm summer day, Spencer and I drove up to Mama B's house and dropped the kids off for a few hours. We kissed the kids goodbye and took off running together. Typically, when we ran together, I followed Spencer's lead. It was more exciting that way. For this particular run, we ran all the way to our new house, about three miles from Mama B's. From there we headed into the downtown area, which is where we have some of our fondest memories together. For two years before we were engaged, we lived in Cedarburg. So not only was Cedarburg going to be our hometown soon, it already was years ago!

Outside of childcare while Spencer and I went on runs together, which wasn't often, I had to call on family for help just so I could complete my individual runs. I'm sure you're familiar with the saying, "It takes a village." This is especially true when running a marathon.

Spencer is the founder and CEO of his own company, and his travel schedule is incredibly busy at times. Travel inevitably shakes up our routine. When Spence was gone, I would keep up with my full-time job while also caring for the kids and keeping up with my training. This was overwhelming to say the least.

I'd wonder to myself, *How do I juggle this marathon training, without getting sores, while keeping up with work, while also caring for the kids, while my husband isn't home?* It's easy with a village like ours! At times, I felt like I was walking a tightrope, balancing a pencil on my nose while juggling eggs. It was a fine line, and I was balancing a lot. But our village made this, and so many other things, possible!

When Spencer was traveling, my mom and dad were just a call away if ever I needed their help with the kids so I could get my training in. My cousin Catherine and her husband, Eric, even stepped in a few times to come over and play with the kids while I went out to run.

And here's a twist: with Spencer's frequent travel, the kids and I would pick up and go with him sometimes. Traveling with two toddlers and a baby was possibly trickier than the actual training for the marathon, but we did it to ensure we still had our family time, even in the midst of our busy times. With every one of those trips, I remained steadfast in my training. This was only made possible as at least one of our parents would come along on the trip as well. Having them there made it possible for me to carve time out each day to train. Even while Spencer was working thirteen-hour days. Even while we were away from home. I stuck to it, no matter what!

As training continued throughout the summer, I started a new practice on my long runs, which brought immense purpose and meaning to all the time I was spending while running. As soon as I started running ten or more miles, I would write names on my forearms with a permanent marker. Then I would dedicate each mile to the person listed next to that number on my arm.

I would think about them, reminisce on memories we had together, and pray for them. In my prayers, for every single person written on my arm, I'd thank God for blessing me with that person's presence in my life. I reflected on the role they played and how they impacted me. These dedications throughout each mile kept me humble and thankful. They reminded me that each moment, each stride, was a gift.

The Chicago Marathon 2023 was scheduled to take place on Sunday, October 8. This made for an eventful summer in 2023. By the end of the summer, my long runs consisted of up to sixteen miles at a time. After accomplishing each long run, I felt more prepared and free. However, the longer the runs, the more post-run recovery my amputated leg required. Part of my training consisted of experimenting with the distance I could run before I needed to readjust the inner liner of my prosthetic.

When I first started training, I was happy if I made it two miles at a time before needing to stop for an adjustment. By September, one month prior to the race, I could go thirteen to fifteen miles without making one adjustment. As I was determined to last longer in between "leg stops," I found myself pushing through pain in my stump (amputated leg) just to finish my mileage. While this was an important piece of my training plan, it caused me to push myself too far at times. I'd feel the harsh burn of dry silicone rubbing on my stump, but I'd push through, trying to make it more and more miles in between stopping to adjust my prosthetic.

After my eighteen-mile run just before Labor Day, five weeks before marathon day, I noticed a slight sore afterward. But I didn't slow down. I continued with a very busy Labor Day. Our weekend consisted of hosting a three-in-one party, with almost a hundred attendees. This party served three purposes: Teddy's third birthday celebration, the Green Bay Packers Season Opener watch party, and also our Farewell to Kenosha, Wisconsin (our hometown at the time) as we were moving into our new home in Cedarburg just five days after the marathon.

In addition to hosting this party, we golfed as a family and spent two days in Cedarburg. We walked several miles around town for various family activities. I was in the moment, enjoying the kids and Spencer. I didn't take any extra no-leg time that weekend, but I was pushing through pain. The pain continued to get worse.

Since my focus is always very happily pulled to my kids and their needs, I hardly ever take time to pull off my prosthetic and check it out when I feel pain. On the day after Labor Day, I finally took the time to evaluate what was going on with my stump. The sore from my last long run was puffy and red. The opening was larger and deeper than the last time I had looked, and of course it was more painful. When I sent a picture of it to my doctor, he referred me to see a wound clinic, but the clinic didn't have any openings until after the marathon. I was in trouble. I had no choice but to completely stop wearing my prosthetic for a few days to allow the sore to heal.

Not wearing my prosthetic meant no running, no biking, and severe limitations in my strength and mobility exercises. *Could this be the end of my marathon journey?* I thought to myself. *Maybe this is not meant to be.* Yet I still felt a fire inside. I wanted this so badly. I couldn't let this stop me. I didn't come all this way just to pull out at the end. I couldn't help but hear my old trainer's voice in my head. I just had to prove him wrong. I had to prove to myself that I could do it.

My new training plan consisted of swimming. Lots of swimming. I despised the idea of swimming at the time, as swimming was the only exercise I could do when I was going through limb salvage. So, when I had my new abilities as an amputee, swimming for fitness was the last thing I wanted to do. Also, when swimming for fitness as an amputee, I completely remove my prosthetic. It is extremely challenging to swim with just my stump. I had to teach the rest of my body how to compensate.

With just weeks remaining until the marathon, I finally got back into my prosthetic and began running again. I could only do short runs, less than one hour, and I began to worry if I would make it in the marathon. When October arrived, I did my last long run before the big race. It was only a ten-mile run, per my training plan. I missed the milestone of my twenty-mile run, which should have occurred the week after Labor Day. This means that the longest run I completed in my training before the marathon was eighteen miles. I wondered what it would feel like to run those extra eight miles on marathon day. No matter what, I was ready to try my best.

EXERCISE: Train Your Attitude[11]

Explore the following three ways to train your attitude. Dedicating this time to strategize will remind you that your attitude is always greater than your circumstances.

1. **GRATITUDE:** Start a gratitude journal. Take a moment each day to write down at least one thing you're grateful for. It's okay if you write the same thing down sometimes—just write what you feel on that particular day! When challenges arise or negative emotions creep in throughout the day, remind yourself of what you wrote in your gratitude journal. This will inevitably make gratitude your default.
2. **BE HERE NOW:** The only moment you truly have is the one you are currently in. When you are present in the moment, you naturally will feel less stressed and more focused. This will make it easier to allow your positive attitude to shine. Practice whichever mindfulness exercises suit you, such as deep breathing, meditating, or yoga. These exercises help bring your mind and body together into the present moment, which is a wonderful place to be.
3. **CONTROL THE CONTROLLABLE:** Focus on what you can control: your thoughts, your actions, and your attitudes. Let go of the rest. When challenges arise, take a moment to journal which pieces are within your control and which pieces are not. Then focus your energy and mind only on the pieces you can control. Put actionable steps into place to move forward positively.

---

[11] Mike Oppland, scientifically reviewed by Christina R. Wilson, "13 Most Popular Gratitude Exercises & Activities," PositivePsychology.com, April 28, 2017, https://positivepsychology.com/gratitude-exercises.

In the final days leading up to the marathon, I focused on maintaining a positive attitude, no matter the circumstances. I was manifesting in my mind a visual of myself running the marathon and crossing that finish line. Nothing was going to stop me! Everything I had overcome up until this point in my life has conditioned me far beyond any of the actual marathon training. I was ready.

CHAPTER 10

MARATHON MENTALITY

"Turn your obstacles into opportunities and your problems into possibilities."
—Roy T. Bennett

When you think about running a marathon, what comes to mind? Personally, I think about goals. If you want to run a marathon, your overarching goal is to run the marathon. To train for that marathon and cross the finish line, you must define small, attainable steps to get there. You must dare to dream while also being realistic and giving yourself grace when things don't go as planned. This same logic likely applies to the goals you recorded in the goal-setting exercise you completed in chapter 2. Go back to that exercise and highlight the goals that scare you the most. Let's lean into those. What would happen if you pursued them? What would it feel like if you achieved them?

I'm sure you've heard the metaphor, "Life is a marathon, not a sprint." Let's break that down for a moment. When we envision life as a marathon, we're acknowledging its enduring nature. A marathon is not a brief, intense burst of effort like a sprint, but rather a long-distance race that demands sustained endurance, perseverance, and resilience. Similarly, life presents us with a series of challenges, obstacles, and opportunities that require consistent effort and commitment over an extended period.

This is exactly what I'm referring to when I say "marathon mentality." To envision going through life with sustained endurance, perseverance, and resilience despite the challenges and obstacles is to have marathon mentality. This exact mentality is what has gotten me to where I am today.

October 8, 2023, is a day I will never forget. I set my alarm for five a.m. to allow for plenty of time before the race. Spencer and I settled into a hotel in downtown Chicago the night before. We even brought our three sons with us and snuggled up with them for our last sleep before the race. The kids were so excited to have a big family sleepover; little did they know what we were in for the next day. When my alarm buzzed at five a.m., I hopped out of bed immediately. No pun intended.

I crawled to the bathroom very quietly and successfully snuck in a shower before anyone else woke up. Spencer and I both got ready and headed out the door before any of the kids woke up. I will never forget the feeling I had that day. I woke up feeling excited, nervous, anxious, but ready. My heart was racing, and I couldn't sit still. I couldn't wait for the race to begin.

Spencer and I fundraised for the nonprofit organization known as GLASA, which stands for Great Lakes Adaptive Sports Association. As I previously shared, I was fortunate to become involved with GLASA very early on after my amputation. They provided my first opportunity to compete again, in track and field! I was thrilled to be running in the Chicago Marathon for Team GLASA.

GLASA hosted pre-race and post-race hospitality in the ballroom of our hotel. We joined them for breakfast before the race. Beginning our day surrounded by so many incredible people who were about to embark on the same journey was inspiring, to say the least. We all were together on one mission to represent and raise funds for GLASA. The funds raised that day provided athletic opportunities to those with different abilities than us. For me, as an amputee, I wasn't just running for myself. I was also running to represent and to give hope to fellow amputees.

I once was laughed at for having the crazy thought that my quality of life could be more. Many times, I was told no: You can't do that; you can only do this. I once was told "someone like me" shouldn't run a marathon, at least not this year. And there I was, ready to run. I was determined to take every stride in that race as an embodiment of GLASA's mission: "Let no one sit on the sidelines." I've been on the sidelines for far too long, and now my chance to jump back in the game had finally arrived. As Spencer and I left the hotel and made our way to the starting line, all I could think was one thing: *Let's go!*

Just before the race began, Spencer and I were surrounded by fellow runners. The energy in the air was remarkable, unlike anything I had experienced before. Spencer and I committed to sticking together throughout the whole race; we thought it would be more fun that way. And it was! Spencer and I trained at a similar pace, and all along he was planning to stick by my side throughout the entire race, even if I needed a stop for my leg. Finally, the race began. The cheers and the crowd were booming. I couldn't believe I was in such an extraordinary moment. Wow.

As it often happens, especially with rookie marathoners, we started out of the gate at a faster pace than what we had trained at all year. I kept reminding Spencer that we should slow down and pace ourselves, but he encouraged me to just be in the moment and ride the wave. We did a combination of both.

Throughout the entire race, people would tap me on the shoulder and give me a thumbs-up, applaud, or tell me that I'm inspiring. When this first happened, it caught me off guard. As a woman ran past me, she tapped me on the shoulder and shouted, "You're amazing, keep it up!" I immediately responded, "Thank you, you're amazing too!" as I thought to myself how nice she was. Then I realized, *Oh yeah, I'm an amputee. And I'm running a marathon. I guess that is amazing!*

I was humbled and proud all at the same time. Every moment throughout the race, I reflected on my journey. I thought about the pain and fears I had overcome. I thought about the blood, sweat, and tears that led me to this moment. I remembered how lucky I was to be where I was. A tremendous sense of gratitude filled me that day. I don't think there was a moment during that race where I wasn't smiling. It was a dream come true.

I had a member of GLASA's coaching staff on call that day, circling the course with a backpack of some of my extra leg supplies. Although I planned and trained for only one leg stop at mile fifteen, it was reassuring to know I could stop for a tune-up anywhere if needed. I'm happy to say that I made

MARATHON MENTALITY

it there for my first and only leg stop. At mile fifteen, not only were my leg supplies awaiting me but so was the best cheering squad ever. Our sons, Gordon, Teddy, and Jackson, along with our village of support were all there to greet us as I sat down to quickly switch out part of my prosthetic.

I would not have been able to run in this marathon without Spencer by my side, without the motivation my kids so effortlessly gave me each day, and without the support of my family and friends. On marathon day, my village consisted of my kids, my parents, two of my brothers, my mother-in-law, and my cousin and her husband.

The main reason for my stop was to switch out my silicone liner, which is the inner-most piece of my prosthetic. After running fifteen miles, due to sweat and swelling, I planned to switch to a fresh, cold liner. So I put my extra liner in a cooler and sent it with our village to meet at mile fifteen. As I switched out my liner, Gordon assisted by holding my running blade. I remember stopping what I was doing and just looking into his eyes, feeling proud. I thought to myself, *How did I get so lucky?*

As I hurried to finish up with my prosthetic, I thought about how much I loved being a mom. No matter what I did in life, just knowing I had three little boys (and Spencer) to share it with, made every single experience better. And just like that, the leg stop was over. I hugged and kissed the kids as I ran off. "See you at the finish line!" I shouted. Just eleven more miles to go.

Aside from hugging and kissing the kids at my leg stop, there are two pieces of the race that were my favorite. First, Spencer's energy was the absolute best. I had to reserve an extra bit of energy each mile just to keep up while laughing. Running while laughing is actually very challenging. Spencer was full of jokes and silly comments. The most hilarious thing he did was run up to the crowds of people cheering and raising his hands up at them, as if every person's sole purpose in that crowd was to cheer for him. And the best part is, he did this multiple times and it was equally hilarious each time.

Second, on a more serious note, I had very special dedications written on my arms on race day. The most significant characters in my story of life were written on my arms. They gave me motivation, peace, and fuel for the entire 26.2 miles. To each person written on my arm on marathon day, thank you. Thank you for the extra push of motivation on that day. But more importantly, thank you for the impact you've had, and continue to have, in my life.

As I approached mile twenty, I felt pain in my left hip. Surprisingly, my amputated leg was doing great. Although, physically seeing my stump at the leg stop did get in my head for a bit. It didn't hurt, but it looked like it did. My stump was oddly shaped, puffy, and bright red. The scars across the bottom were dark purple. I began to worry if my leg went numb and I couldn't feel the pain.

Very quickly, however, I vanished the thought of worry from my mind. I very intentionally stopped thinking about my pain. Instead, I let my mind settle on all the positive things. Spencer right beside me. The cheers, smiles, and signs in the crowd. At several points in the marathon, I deliberately tried to read every single sign I passed.

This was one of those points where I focused on reading the signs. And then the most amazing wave of thoughts and emotions filled me. I realized right then and there I was coping. What I was doing was challenging. It was causing me pain. And there I was, using my mind to give me the power I needed to push through.

MARATHON MENTALITY

When we turned the corner onto Michigan Avenue, the final stretch, I already started celebrating in my mind. *You did it!* I thought, with the finish line so close. As much as my body was ready for the race to end, I thought to myself that I didn't want it to end. To this day, I still replay memories from the race in my head. It was an amazing journey. With the finish line in sight, Spencer and I picked up our pace as my legs felt heavier and heavier with every stride. We approached the finish line and grabbed each other's hands. We did it! As we crossed the finish line hand-in-hand, tears filled my eyes, and the greatest sense of joy filled my entire body.

One word I would use to describe the feeling I had after crossing that finish line is *euphoric*. Of course, in addition to the euphoric feeling, I felt fatigue and a bit of pain. It was challenging to walk in my running blade as the blade is mounted higher than my other leg so that my hips would be level while running. Especially after finishing a marathon, walking in my running blade was even more challenging. Thankfully, I quickly spotted a wheelchair nearby and collapsed into it as a race aid pushed me along.

I kept thinking to myself, *Did I really just do that? Me? I ran a marathon?* And as the euphoric "I just crossed the finish line" feeling wore off, I was yet again consumed with gratitude. I was thankful for every step in my journey that led me to exactly where I was in that moment. In a wheelchair. Rolling through Grant Park. Just after crossing the finish line of the Chicago Marathon. What a beautiful moment in life.

The personal growth that comes along with running a marathon is such a gift. Running a marathon creates an opportune moment to learn and exercise some of life's greatest lessons. It begins with the months of training leading up to the marathon. The experience is packed with opportunities to learn. You learn how to persevere. You learn how to overcome adversity. You learn to take care of yourself. You learn what you are capable of. And then when you step up to that starting line to run 26.2 miles, you are given the opportunity to exercise all those learnings as you take each stride toward the finish line. And then when you cross the finish line, you are rewarded with the feelings of accomplishment, fulfillment, strength, and gratitude.

Life is a marathon, not a sprint.

In life, we are given opportunities to learn and exercise those learnings, just like I did when running a marathon. In life, the greatest opportunities to learn often arrive when unforeseen things happen, or when we are challenged with adversity. Perspective plays a significant role in what we learn and when we learn it.

When adversity hits, if we are too busy feeling sorry for ourselves, we may completely overlook the life lesson that is right in front of us. On the contrary, if we have a positive perspective, we take on the power to find the exact learnings we need. If we embrace those learnings, we will absorb them. And when we absorb those learnings, we find the opportunities to exercise them. This is where resilience comes in.

We must be resilient enough to continue exercising those life lessons we've gathered, no matter what our circumstances may be. We must be resilient enough to continue finding those life lessons hiding behind diversity. It is up to us. The power is in our hands to own our attitudes, shatter our limits, and live a triumphant life.

EXERCISE: 30-Day Challenge

Reference the goals you highlighted in your chapter 2 goals list. These should be the goals that scare you the most. Choose at least one of those goals to focus on for the next thirty days. Complete the 30-Day Challenge template below to set yourself up for success in achieving your goal(s). If you're struggling to decide which goals to fit into your 30-Day Challenge, here are some examples:

- Commit to daily exercise, twenty minutes per day of doing some form of exercise.
- Focus on your sleep routine, going to bed and waking up around the same time every day.
- For thirty minutes every day read a book, article, or anything that interests you.
- Commit to daily positive affirmations to boost self-confidence and positivity.
- Declutter one area of your home every day.
- Journal for ten to twenty minutes every day.
- Perform random acts of kindness every day.
- Try a no-spend challenge, where you avoid non-essential spending.

The opportunities are endless!

NOTE: You may complete this activity for one goal at a time or for multiple goals at one time.

| 30-Day Challenge | Start Date: |

Goal:	I want this because:

How am I going to achieve this goal?

MARATHON MENTALITY

Specific Tasks:	Complete By:

How did it go?

What did I learn?

MARATHON MENTALITY

Optional: Use a Calendar template to mark or track specific activities or milestones.

Year: _____

Month: _____

Sunday	Monday	Tuesday	Wednesday	Thursday	Friday	Sunday
		Notes:				

CONCLUSION

"Life isn't about finding yourself. Life is about creating yourself."
—George Bernard Shaw

We have the power to influence our reality. When reflecting on my own story, I wanted to identify one key factor within my own control that drove me to succeed in the ways I have. That factor is the title of this book: Perspective Is Power!

I have gone from unstable to unstoppable, from victim to victorious, and I truly attribute this to my ability to use perspective in my favor. Undoubtedly, I've had a fair share of trauma and hardship very early in life. With so much life left to live, each hardship better prepared me for the other challenges thrown my way. Today I live with the anticipation that there will be hardship in my future. Isn't it true that *everyone* has challenges and that *nothing* is perfect? Standing firm with my positive attitude, I believe anything is possible and I will overcome anything. Nothing will ever stand in my way of living the life of my dreams, as long as I possess the right attitude.

Now the choice is yours. What will you choose? Will hardship and obstacles keep you from living the life of your dreams? It is completely up to you. Turn those obstacles into opportunities. Believe in yourself. Experience those bumps in the road as if they are blessings. See your own challenges as a chance to grow. And above all else, always strive to choose the best possible perspective.

You have the power!

APPENDIX A

LIZ'S QUOTE BOOK

This section includes a listing of quotes near and dear to me. Throughout my journey, I would see or hear brilliant, inspiring quotes and write them down or post them on display around my home. I hope you enjoy these bits of inspiration as much as I have.

Overcoming Adversity & Resilience

- "Do not let what you cannot do interfere with what you can do." —John Wooden
- "Sometimes the bad things that happen in our lives put us directly on the path to the best things that will ever happen to us." —Nicole Reed
- "Life doesn't get easier or more forgiving; we get stronger and more resilient." —Steve Maraboli
- "Persistence and resilience only come from having been given the chance to work through difficult problems." —Gever Tulley
- "Obstacles don't have to stop you. If you run into a wall, don't turn around and give up. Figure out how to climb it. Go through it, or work around it." —Michael Jordan

- "Your hardest times often lead to the greatest moments of your life. Keep going. Tough situations build strong people in the end." —Roy T. Bennett
- "Press forward. Do not stop, do not linger in your journey, but strive for the mark set before you." —George Whitefield

Growth & Transformation

- "10% of life is made up of what happens to you, and 90% is determined by how you react to those events." —Steven Covey
- "Every day, you reinvent yourself. You're always in motion. But you decide every day: forward or backward." —James Altucher
- "When things are bad, it's the best time to reinvent yourself." —George Lopez
- "The real self is not something one finds as much as it is something one makes." —Sydney J. Harris
- "Changing your perspective changes your experience." —Paul McGregor
- "Reality is a question of perspective." —Salman Rushdie
- "Everything is either an opportunity to grow or an obstacle to keep you from growing. You get to choose." —Wayne Dyer

Faith & Belief

- "Whether you think you can, or you think you can't—you're right." —Henry Ford

CONCLUSION

- "If you lose money you lose much, if you lose friends you lose more, if you lose faith you lose all." —Eleanor Roosevelt
- "A sign of wisdom is believing you're limitless, because you are." —Maxime Lagacé
- "There are only two ways to live your life. One is as though nothing is a miracle. The other is as though everything is a miracle." —Albert Einstein
- "Belief bends reality." —Kinoko Nasu
- "Whatever it is you believe about yourself, that is what others will believe about you too." —Harvey Volson

Mindset & Perspective

- "Your perspective will either become your prison or your passport." —Steven Furtick
- "Our attitude toward life determines life's attitude toward us." —John Mitchell
- "A positive attitude gives you power over your circumstances instead of your circumstances having power over you." —Brian Ford
- "If you change the way you look at things, the things you look at change." —Wayne Dyer

Empowerment & Taking Action

- "You want to be in the driver's seat of your own life because if you are not, life will drive you." —Oprah Winfrey
- "Show up in every single moment like you're meant to be there." —Marie Forleo
- "Onward and upward." —Lev Grossman

- "Turn your obstacles into opportunities and your problems into possibilities." —Roy T. Bennett

Motivation, Encouragement & Hope

- "In the end, everything will be okay. If it's not okay, it's not the end." —Unknown
- "That which does not kill us makes us stronger." —Friedrich Nietzsche
- "Life is like riding a bicycle. To keep your balance, you must keep moving." —Albert Einstein
- "Press forward. Do not stop. Do not linger in your journey, but strive for the mark set before you." —George Whitefield

APPENDIX B

RESOURCES

To learn more about The Great Lakes Adaptive Sports Association (GLASA), read below and visit https://GLASA.org.

These are the great things GLASA does . . .

- Provides Lifelong Pursuit of Health and Wellness
    - GLASA believes that health is a lifelong pursuit and offers programs for individuals ages three to over seventy-five. GLASA supports athletes with primary physical or visual disabilities, such as amputation, cerebral palsy, dwarfism, muscular dystrophy, spinal cord injury, spina bifida, stroke, visual impairment, and more.

- Develops and Delivers Adaptive Programming to Fit Every Need
    - GLASA's programs are adapted to meet the needs of individuals who use manual or power wheelchairs in addition to those with ambulatory disabilities. They also offer specialized programming to injured military veterans.
- Ensures No One Sits on the Sidelines
    - No one is ever turned away due to an inability to pay, and no prior experience is needed to join GLASA recreational or competitive programs. With twenty-plus adaptive sports to get involved with, there is something for everyone.

CONCLUSION

One other amazing nonprofit worth mentioning is 50 Legs Foundation. 50 Legs partners with Prosthetic and Orthotic Associates (POA) and makes possibilities become reality for countless amputees. To learn more about 50 Legs, read below and visit https://50legs.org.

A note from the 50 Legs Foundation . . .

The 50 Legs team is made up primarily of volunteers and a few staff—many of us have prosthetics or have family members with prosthetics. We know you have hopes, dreams, and goals, and money shouldn't stand in the way of your freedom. You can live your best possible life with properly fitted prosthetics, and it's our honor to make that happen for you. While you're at one of our trusted provider locations for your appointment, a member of our team will reach out to meet with you. We'll also connect you with any resources or support services you need now and in the future.

ACKNOWLEDGMENTS

- My amazing publishing team at Selfpublishing.com, especially Karen Pina
- My brilliant editing team at Catt Editing, LLC, especially Carly Catt
- My very talented photographer, Tara Fay
- My Village
    - The loves of my life: Spencer, Gordon, Teddy, and Jackson
    - My parents: Joe and Sheri Clark
    - My siblings: Joey, Fur, Jay, and Kara Clark
    - My grandparents, may they rest in peace: Papa (Jerome) and Nana (Gwen Coniker), Servant of God, Grandpa Ed Clark and Grandma Rita Clark
    - My bonus family: Mama B (Beth Bursten), Lindsey and Joseph Clark III, Bill and Dolores Bursten, Tyler, Sarah, Penny, and Charlie Bursten
    - My medical providers, especially Dr. David DelToro, Dr. William Ertl, Dr. Aaron Morgan, Dr. Anthony Park, Dr. Aida Shanti, Dr. Winthrop, and Heidi Conto, LCSW, CEDS-C, CIR, RM
    - My dear cousins, especially Cynthia Bennett and Catherine Dame

- The Saint Joseph High School (SJHS) community, especially Mrs. McTernan, Mrs. Hildreth, and Mr. Maki
- The SJHS girls tennis community, especially coaches Rick and Gail Bedore
- The Saint Mary's College and Concordia University of Wisconsin communities, especially Professor Jahns
- My work family, you know who you are!
- The Stefanie Joseph Memorial Fund (SJMF) family, especially Lynn and Katherine Hill
- The Prosthetic and Orthotic Associates family, especially Stan Patterson, Roger Underhill, and Ronnie Dickson
- The Great Lakes Adaptive Sports Association (GLASA) family, especially Cindy and Randy Housner, Dave Bogenschutz (may he rest in peace), and Kelly Candotti Habas
- The Saint Anne's family, especially Deacon Rich Stanula
- All amazing friends and family who have been there, you know who you are!

ABOUT THE AUTHOR

Elizabeth (Liz) Bursten lives in Cedarburg, Wisconsin, with her loving husband, Spencer, and three beautifully energetic sons, Gordon, Theodore (Teddy), and Jackson. Aside from caring for her family, Liz works in process improvement for a top ten global pharmaceutical company. In her free time, Liz enjoys spending time with family and friends, entertaining, traveling, and staying active through biking, running, golfing, and keeping up with her kids. "I love the opportunity my sons give me to relive my childhood through playing with toys, building Legos, doing arts and crafts, and playing all sorts of games."

Liz is passionate about uplifting the adaptive community. She believes in living by example, showcasing that you can live an active and abundant life, even with physical impairments. Liz has enjoyed partnering with and fundraising for GLASA over the years and looks forward to continuing to impact the adaptive community throughout her life.

HELP ME TO HELP OTHERS

To book a speaking engagement or to learn more about Liz, visit https://lizbursten.com.

selfpublishing.com helped me, and now I want them to help you with their **FREE book outline template!**

Even if you're busy, bad at writing, or don't know where to start, you CAN write a bestseller and build your best life.

With tools and experience across a variety of niches and professions, selfpublishing.com is the <u>only</u> resource you need to take your book to the finish line!

DON'T WAIT

Say "YES" to becoming a bestseller:

<u>https://selfpublishing.com/friend/</u>

Made in the USA
Columbia, SC
12 July 2025

1b64414d-fc29-4129-bae0-40e4e43de142R02